Gooseberry Patch

Comfort & Joy

Gooseberry Patch

A Country Store In Your Mailbox®

Gooseberry Patch
600 London Road
Department Book
Delaware, OH 43015

★

1·800·854·6673
www.gooseberrypatch.com

Copyright 2004, Gooseberry Patch 1-931890-43-9
Second Printing, August 2004

Do you have a tried & true recipe, tip, craft
or memory that you'd like to see featured in a
Gooseberry Patch book? Please send 'em to us at:

Gooseberry Patch
Attn: Book Dept.
P.O. Box 190
Delaware, OH 43015

P.S. Don't forget to include your name & address!
If we select your recipe, your name will
appear right along with it...and you'll
receive a FREE copy of the book!

Table of Contents

ENJOY!

Dedication

To everyone who delights in the simple joys of the holidays...warm, woolly mittens, a hot cup of cocoa and freshly baked cinnamon rolls on Christmas morning.

Appreciation

To all of you who generously shared your families' fondest Christmas memories and tastiest recipes, our heartfelt thanks!

Shelley Messenger
Russell, MA

When my dad was a child in the 1940's, he and his siblings would write down their lists of wishes for Santa Claus on pieces of paper. They would then tear up the lists, sprinkle the pieces in the fireplace, run outside quickly and watch as the smoke rose from the chimney, magically sending their Christmas lists on the way to Santa. This memory always makes me smile.

Patricia Van Wyk
Newton, IA

When I was growing up, my mother always made cinnamon rolls for our Christmas morning breakfast. She arranged the rolls in the shape of either a Christmas tree or a wreath on a cookie sheet. As the rolls came out of the oven, she would drizzle them with a thin powdered sugar icing, sprinkle them with green sugar crystals and place a shiny red maraschino cherry in the center of each roll. We children thought this was the most festive and tasty treat. Mom never baked one, there was always a second one to be given to a neighbor or friend for their holiday merriment.

Once Upon a Christmas

Brad Daugherty
Gooseberry Patch

Growing up, my parents gave my older brother and myself wonderful, magical Christmases, every year, complete with package upon package piled under the tree. Glittering tinsel draped from what seemed like every corner added sparkle to the constant aroma of cookies and fresh evergreen. My mom was a stay-at-home mom, taking what would be a 12-year absence from teaching elementary school in order to be with us, her children. When I turned 10, she decided to return to teaching first grade. That year, as the holiday approached, I noticed there were presents under the tree addressed to my mom from my dad and vice versa. My parents had usually exchanged a gift or 2, but I had never seen so many! When I asked my dad why, he said, "Because we have more money this year." At the time I didn't fully understand, simply happy that they were happy. Years later, I finally comprehend the magnitude of that moment: for 12 years they sacrificed showing their love for each other, refraining from gift-giving, in order to make sure their children had everything they could have hoped for, every happiness, every wonderful memory. And now, it is that memory that I think of more than any other, that selfless gesture, that fills me with the true spirit of Christmas.

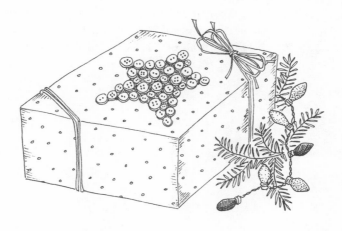

Tina Sheley
Getzville, NY

My favorite childhood memories go back to the days growing up in
the country! My mom always seemed to know when school was going
to be cancelled due to a heavy snow. She encouraged us to stay up
the night before and play board games and cards with her. On these
nights, she would make homemade pizza and set out bowls of
pretzels, crackers and other little snacks. The treats would be our
prizes! She would mix up Shirley Temples for us to sip as we watched
the snow falling while sitting in front of our picture window. Since
Dad worked for the highway department, we guessed how many
times he would have to plow our road that night. Mom always had
a cup of hot cocoa ready for one of us to run out to him every time
he passed our house!

Martha Anderson
Hot Springs, SD

My wrought iron bed stood in a corner of our log cabin living room.
When I was just a little girl, maybe 3 or 4 years old, I remember
waking up on Christmas morning...the newly cut cedar Christmas tree
was full of little candles, all burning bright! Of course, my dad sat
close by with a bucket full of water sitting right beside him. Such a
spectacular sight remains my most beautiful memory of waking up on
that very special day.

Once Upon a Christmas

Fran George
Southfield, MI

My parents were very hard-working people but there was not always extra money for gifts and special things. Christmas, however, was a very important holiday. My father always humbugged at Christmas; he was not a shopper or a spender. But every Christmas, no matter what, there was always a gift just from him for my mother, my sister and myself. It was always such fun to see what he bought each one of us. My dad was the first to give me a string of pearls...I treasure them still.

Kristen Hoopes Openshaw
Taylorsville, UT

Growing up on a dairy farm in snowy Wyoming during the 1960's made for very memorable Christmases! My 3 sisters and I stood at the attic bedroom window early on Christmas mornings where we could see the milking barn windows. When those lights went off, we knew Dad and my brothers were finished milking and would be in to wash up soon. All 8 of us children would line up in the hallway. The youngest peeked into the kitchen to see if Santa had eaten the treats we left out...the next to youngest (ME!) got to look in the living room to see if there were any presents. That was the cue for the fun to begin!

Elizabeth Furry
Minden, NV

One of our favorite traditions every year is to set up our nativity set under the Christmas tree. After we arrange the manger, we put out the animals and Mary & Joseph. Then we put the Wise Men in another part of the house and take turns moving them closer and closer to the manger each day as Christmas approaches…after all, the Wise Men traveled from afar! The kids love to do this and it is fun to see where the Wise Men appear. Sometimes they are in the hallway or on top of a bookshelf or even in the kids' bedrooms. On Christmas Eve, we place Jesus in the manger with the Wise Men surrounding him and sing Happy Birthday to Jesus! This tradition keeps our family focused on Jesus throughout the season.

Jenny Klein
Troy, MI

I was an only child and spent most of my holidays with "the grown-ups," but I had a ball being the center of attention! One of my favorite Christmas memories was of visiting my aunt's and uncle's home about half an hour away. My uncle was an excellent musician. He had a beautiful electric organ in their home and would sit down and play Christmas carols for me…much to my delight! He would use the foot pedals to add background sounds like car horns and train whistles, too. That organ could imitate brass or string instruments. It was wonderful! Our family loved his music, singing carols and eating my grandma's beautifully decorated Christmas cookies.

Once Upon a Christmas

Denise Gidaro
Baden, PA

We spent every Christmas Eve at Grandma's. Her table was filled with great Italian dishes, good conversation and close relatives. One year, as we sat down to dinner, Grandma handed me a pen and told me to write my name on her linen tablecloth! She insisted I sign and pass the pen along to the others. The following Christmas Eve, I noticed she had embroidered all our names on that cloth with brightly colored thread. Even though several family members were not there that year, their names reminded us of many good times. Each of us will forever have a special place at our family dinner table. Years have gone by, yet we use that same tablecloth. This year, the tablecloth is well over 20 years old and we still each have our "special" place at the table!

Henrietta Loveland
Baltimore, MD

As a little girl I can remember going to my grandparents' house to help bake Christmas cookies. Mother would tell my brother and me to come to Grandmother's house right after school that day. All day long while in school I would be daydreaming about baking cookies. We would eat supper and then start baking the delicious butter cookies. Grandmother always gave my mother more than half of the fresh-baked cookies to take home, but when we would visit, she always had plenty of cookies for us there, too! I looked forward to this time every year.

Brandie Pinard
Pittsfield, NH

When I was a child, my family faithfully attended Christmas Eve church service. On the way home, my sister and I would hope to spot Santa in the cold, dark New Hampshire sky. Before retiring, we were each allowed to open just one present...an "appetizer" for what was to come the next morning! We were tucked into our beds, and it never failed that as soon as the hallway light clicked off, my sister would sneak down the hall so we could try to talk one another into sleep. We spent hours promising each other that whoever woke up first would promptly wake up the other. We still laugh about our late Christmas Eve promises even today!

Brenda Smith
Monroe, IN

My favorite Christmas memory is putting up a small fireplace that was made of cardboard. We lived in a small house and Mom would make hot cocoa for my sister and me while we worked. We would then hang our stockings on our fireplace with shiny tacks. We would color in front of that lighted fireplace, sing carols and tell each other stories!

Michelle Bagby
Templeton, CA

Every year we have our friends and their children over before Christmas. We have dinner, read a Christmas story, and then we all go outside and sprinkle "Magic Reindeer Food" on the ground to guide Santa's reindeer to our home. A package full of oatmeal, a little bit of tempera paint and a good dose of glitter goes home with everyone. We all know those magical reindeer can't resist Magic Reindeer Food!

Once Upon a Christmas

Sonia Daily
Midland, MI

We lived in England for several years and one Christmas custom we adopted was the "Christmas cracker." We spent one Christmas Eve with a British family who made their own "crackers" and have continued the tradition even when we moved back to the United States. Each year we decorate the cracker into a different shape. One year they were all made from small paper tubes and were candles, another year wrapped up like gift boxes. We place a small gift or toy inside the container, add a popper noise maker, a paper crown and a Bible verse (instead of a fortune). We open our crackers after Christmas dinner.

Ann Laughlin
Conneaut, OH

I am a third-grade teacher and begin the Christmas season by placing a small (3 to 4-inch) artificial Christmas tree on each of my students' desks. I invite them to bring small items from home to decorate their trees. They never fail to impress me with their ingenuity, bringing in old costume jewelry, buttons, doilies and an assortment of small items, often sharing with friends. Then, after reading *"The Legend of the Christmas Spider"* we make little golden spiders from jingle bells and wire and place them on our trees. I surprise the youngsters while they are outside for recess by putting golden angel hair around each spider, just as the story goes. Their expressions of delight upon returning will always be one of my favorite Christmas memories!

April Hale
Kirkwood, NY

Since I am a working mom, I start to bake my Christmas cookies early and freeze them. Every year, our freezer in the potting shed is full of cookies ready to be packed and shared as gifts. One year just before Christmas, knowing I had all my cookie baking done, I went out to the shed to bring in the cookies to wrap. In the middle of the floor sat an ice chest with paint cans surrounding it. The old coffee pot from our camper sat to the side along with quite a stack of dirty coffee cups. Not a cookie was to be found in that old freezer. When my sons were questioned, I discovered that when they and their friends were outside playing and had gotten cold, they would go to the shed for some warm coffee and yummy cookies! They are grown now and one of the friends is in the military. We still send care packages to them full of those favorite cookies and memories.

Jennifer Ozanich
Flushing, MI

The week before Christmas, we held a progressive-style caroling party! We invited several families and each was simply told to prepare a dessert to share, and to wait. My husband, our 4 children and I left the house and went to the first house, where we sang. That family grabbed their dessert and coats and followed us in our car to the next house, and so on. We were blessed with fresh, fat snowflakes that had fallen all day and continued to fall as we caroled. Snowballs flew at every stop! We ended up with 14 elementary-age kids and almost as many college kids as well as their moms and dads. I'm not sure which group had more fun! We ended the evening sharing hot cocoa and yummy desserts at our home. It was the easiest and perhaps most enjoyable party our family has hosted. We are all looking forward to a repeat next year!

Once Upon a Christmas

Peggy Shaw
Kuna, ID

Growing up in a large family with quite a few children, there wasn't much money for treats. My mother was very busy with so many of us that she didn't make dessert very often. One snowy winter's day when I was very young, my grandmother came over with a real treat. She mixed a couple cups of cold, thick cream with some vanilla and 2 cups sugar, stirring until the sugar dissolved. She then stirred in 2 cups coconut and put the bowl to the side. Outside she went into the snowstorm and gathered up a huge, heaping bowl of freshly fallen snow. She poured the cream mixture on top and stirred it all very fast. She spooned it into bowls for each one of us and we gobbled it down. As children, we thought this was just the most awesome, delicious "ice cream" treat!

Barbara Barber
Westerly, RI

Making snow angels and playing Fox and Geese are favorite memories. Being the first one to make footprints in fresh fallen snow was an experience I cherished. I always liked to glimpse unbroken snow from the vantage point of Mom & Dad's upstairs bedroom window. I loved gazing out over the expanse of snow with nary a print in it. The very thought of a neighbor walking across our yard and interrupting that vision motivated me to run out to be the first to make my footprints in that fresh snow!

Rita Wood
East Sparta, OH

Each year my nieces and nephews come and decorate my Christmas tree. They each have to bring one homemade ornament and I make each of them one ornament. They each have a box that their ornaments go in. Every year as we open the boxes, we fondly remember when they made this or that ornament. Soon we are traveling down memory lane 'til the last memory is hung. When they grow older and are on their own, I will give them their boxes for their own trees. My oldest nephew is now 16 years old and my youngest niece is only one year old. I am so very lucky to enjoy the memories all season long.

Brenda Doak
Gooseberry Patch

Being the oldest of 4 siblings at the time (there were more in the years to come!), I was always Mom's helper. Christmas was, needless to say, a very exciting time at our house…the most fun time of the year. One Christmas Eve, I could barely sleep. After dozing off and on, I finally decided it had to be time for waking up and starting the day. I woke up my groggy siblings, and being the "helper" made them all get dressed. As a group, we ventured down the stairs, my siblings still rubbing their sleepy eyes. We checked out the tree and marveled at all the gifts. I then glanced the clock to make sure we could run and wake up Mom & Dad…it was only one a.m.! I had to make everyone march back up the stairs, help put PJ's back on and sneak back into my own bed. Poor kids, I don't even know if they were old enough to still remember…I must have not been more than 10 years old but it is a memory I cherish. My parents were never any the wiser!

☆ Once Upon a Christmas ☆

Karen Petrie
Bethel Park, PA

About 8 years ago, I was watching my nieces and nephews open many, many gifts. We could have easily lost one of them in the frenzy of discarded papers, boxes, ribbons and tissue! Although elated to see the joy in their faces, it saddened me to think of others not even having one brightly wrapped package to savor for hours and finally open. Next year it was to be different. Each child received a gift especially for him or her, but instead of gifts on end, there was also a check to be donated to a charity of the child's choice...remember, they were young and it had to be made fun. For example, one nephew loves to eat so he was given gift certificates to some of his favorite food chains...but he in turn then used his other half of the gift to feed a dozen homeless men a turkey dinner at our local shelter. An animal-loving niece received a large stuffed animal because she chose to send her gift to Animal Friends. It has expanded to the adults. Our family gardener was given new gloves and a few tools while crops were planted in Guatemala in her name. A new red sweater came with a donation to Project Bundle-Up and so the years have gone by. We've donated to river conservation, children and family services, art councils and a bottle of Wild Turkey came with adoption of a live turkey at a local aviary!

It is fun and feels so good (twice!). Now many of the kids pick their own charity. I've even sent a signed check when we haven't gotten together, for them to fill in the name of the recipient. Will it come back with their name or a charity? It has always, proudly, been the charity. It is always better to give than to receive.

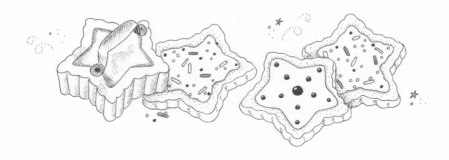

Barbara Voight
Duluth, MN

Every year my family went to my grandpa's farm in the backwoods of northeastern Wisconsin about 2 weeks before Christmas. My mother and Gramma packed thermoses full of hot cocoa, sandwiches made with Gramma's home-baked buns and cookies for dessert. Then Grampa and my father hooked up the big bobsled to the tractor. We all rode on the sled for a whole day of picking and chopping down Christmas trees. We picked ours, theirs, my other grandparents' as well as one for every classroom in my school…even a very large tree for our school gym! We all climbed up on top of the pile of trees and rode the bobsled home. The next day, my father delivered 7 of the trees to my school. He carried them in, one at a time, and built a wooden stand for each one. Then he took them to the classrooms. My teacher let me go and help until all the trees were set up. We waited and put the huge one up in the gym last. Our family was very poor, but on that day I felt so important and so very proud of my father!

Nita Pilkington
Branson West, MO

Our holiday tradition is that gifts cannot be bought brand-new, they must be homemade or from a craft store, yard sale or flea market! My grandmother started the tradition and my mother, myself, my daughter and now my granddaughters are keeping the tradition going. These little surprises make our Christmas even more special to each one of us.

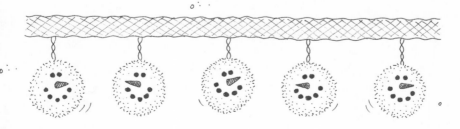

Once Upon a Christmas

Virginia Hagerman
Jolo, WV

My family are Christmas Crazies! We start celebrating the Saturday after Thanksgiving by writing out our Christmas cards. We then have a party every weekend until Christmas. They all have a theme and we even give away door prizes! Last year we had a snowflake card party and decorated old mailboxes to store our cards in. In the past we have each decorated a door in my grandparents' house! The season doesn't end until New Year's Eve with a movie, game playing and pizza party. Last year we had a food basket contest. We are a family of 25 and every Christmas Eve is spent at my grandparents' house. We have even made wreaths to go all along our fence. All of this started when my husband and I first married and had our first child. Money was tight and we couldn't afford a lot of decorations. The relatives showed up and we made them...paper chains and popcorn strings! Now, 7 years later, we are already making plans for this Christmas.

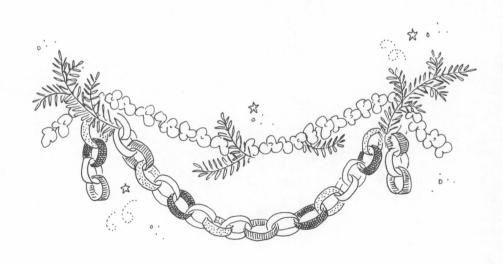

Leslie Stimel
Gooseberry Patch

Every year as a child, on the evening after Thanksgiving, my sisters and I would get bundled up in our snowsuits, hats and mittens, then load into the car with our mom & dad for a drive into town. We were always so excited to watch the historic county courthouse come alive with colorful lights and holiday decorations in a celebration that brought people together from miles around. I remember standing in the crisp, cool night, singing Christmas carols with the rest of the crowd and waiting for Santa to arrive. Soon, a big, red fire truck would come rolling around the town square and perched on top was a jolly Santa, waving to the children and ready to usher in the holiday season with the lighting of the courthouse. He'd climb up the front steps and ask us if we'd all been naughty or nice, then he'd ask us to help him shout "Merry Christmas!" or "Rudolph!" loud enough to make the lights "magically" turn on. It always took a few tries, but when we shouted loud enough, the beautiful old courthouse would light up with such splendor that it always took my breath away. When I was in my teens, I got to enjoy this special holiday tradition with my three nephews, and I hope to someday share it with my own children too.

Once Upon a Christmas

Marilyn Godfrey
Stephenville, TX

When I was about 12 years old, we traveled to my grandmother's house for the holidays. She did not celebrate Christmas due to religious beliefs but that year she agreed for us to celebrate. Of course, she had no decorations so we first went out to the woods to cut down a tree. In that part of Texas, that meant a scrubby cedar tree. Then we popped popcorn that Grandma had grown in her garden using a long-handled popper over a fire in her fireplace. We busied ourselves stringing the popcorn and making ornaments from aluminum foil, cardboard and greeting cards received throughout the years. Daddy had some fireworks. He took a scoop of coals from the fireplace and piled them on the rocky road outside from which we could light them. That homemade Christmas is still oh-so fresh even though I don't remember a single gift...it was all about family!

Mary Gilbert
Swartz Creek, MI

When my 3 brothers and I were young, my parents would pick a snowy Saturday in December to travel downtown to Belle Isle. We would ice skate until dusk on the Detroit River. Afterwards, we'd eat sandwiches, popcorn and hot chocolate my mom had packed earlier that day. We all enjoyed watching the skaters and sharing our Christmas wishes with each other as we warmed up in the car. We would then drive all around downtown Detroit looking at all the beautiful Christmas decorations in the storefronts. Our favorite was Hudson's Department Store. It rose 12 stories and was lit up as a big Christmas tree. We'd park in front and just stare with wonder. Such a perfect time for more cookies and hot chocolate. We'd sing carols and just have the best ride home. The love in that car could never have been measured...they were the best times of my life.

Once Upon a Christmas

Cyndi Little
Whitsett, NC

I'll never forget the Christmas my friend and I went to purchase our Christmas trees together. Her daughter came along just for the fun of it. After looking at several trees, we each found our perfect tree. A young man tied the trees to the top of my van, assuring us all the while they were secure...very secure. We kept asking him to double-check because in our eyes he was paying much more attention to the beautiful young lady with us than our oh-so-perfect trees. After much teasing and promises of returning with homemade soup for the boys working, we were on our way. We were laughing and enjoying our ride home when we heard this noise...a peek in the mirror justified my horror. Not one, but both trees shot off the top of my van...splintering in the highway! It was one of those horrible yet so funny experiences. We pulled over and cleared the roadway of our trees and then headed right back to the tree lot for 2 more trees. The boys greeted us with open arms and it took some convincing before they believed us. We did end up with 2 more perfect trees and oh, what a fun time we had! The story is shared over and over each year with new details added each time!

Rhonda Webb
Huntington, IN

One Christmas holiday, my daughter decided she would make gelatin jigglers as her contribution to the celebratory meal. She and my oldest daughter went off to purchase the necessities. By the time they arrived home and began, I was busy myself in the kitchen, so I didn't pay much attention to what they were cooking up. Pretty soon it became evident a few mis-measurements had been made. Instead of throwing it all out, the girls put their heads and their calculators together. The solution...purchase 24 *more* boxes of gelatin! The last thing I heard as they went out the door was, "We better go to another store because they were running low."

When they returned, we reheated the first batch and added the new packages. I don't know exactly how many snowmen jigglers we ended up with, but we did have 2 large containers of scraps alone! By the time all was said & done, our refrigerator was overflowing. Thanks to our cold Indiana winters we stored the extras in the car out in the garage! Not wanting to waste anything, we sliced the scrap pieces into cubes, piled them in glass bowls and topped with whipped topping for very special and colorful desserts. We just jiggled these bowls full of joy to all our neighbors!

Good Morning Cheer

100% BREAKFAST

Sweetly Simple Coffee Cake

Jo Ann

A good morning sweet treat.

2 10-oz. tubes refrigerated
   biscuits
1/4 c. margarine, melted

1/3 c. brown sugar, packed
1-1/2 t. cinnamon
1/4 c. chopped nuts

Arrange biscuits very close together in a 9" round cake pan. Mix together margarine, brown sugar, cinnamon, and nuts; spread over biscuits. Bake at 350 degrees for 20 minutes. Serves 8.

Cinnamon-Raisin Breakfast Strips

Julie Montalto
Pembroke Pines, FL

A great grab & go breakfast when teamed with a juice box
or mug of hot cocoa.

2-1/2 c. biscuit baking mix
1/2 c. raisins
1/4 c. plain yogurt

1/2 c. milk
1/2 t. cinnamon

Mix all ingredients until a soft dough forms; knead 5 times. Roll dough into a 10"x6" rectangle; cut into 10, one-inch strips. Place on an ungreased baking sheet; bake at 450 degrees for 10 to 12 minutes. Makes 10.

Good Morning Cheer

Holiday Brunch Casserole

Cathie Sondag
Harlan, IA

Quick & easy to prepare the evening before, then just pop it in the oven in the morning!

2-1/2 c. seasoned croutons
2 c. shredded Cheddar cheese, divided
1-1/2 lb. ground sausage, browned
6 to 8 eggs

2-3/4 c. milk, divided
3/4 t. dry mustard
1/2 t. salt
1/8 t. pepper
10-3/4 oz. can cream of mushroom soup

Arrange croutons in a greased 13"x9" baking pan. Top with 1-1/2 cups shredded cheese, then with sausage. Blend together eggs and 2-1/4 cups milk in a large bowl; add mustard, salt and pepper and mix well. Pour egg mixture over sausage; cover with aluminum foil and refrigerate overnight. Just before baking, blend together remaining milk and soup and pour over egg mixture; sprinkle with remaining cheese. Bake at 350 degrees for one to 1-1/2 hours. Serves 8.

Decorate a small galvanized mailbox with ribbons, buttons and painted-on snowflakes. Add your name to each side with a paint pen in big, bold letters…a whimsical holder for those holiday cards, photos and letters.

Quick & Easy Quiche

Marty Bontumasi
Salisbury, NC

Make this quiche a day or 2 before company's expected and freeze for a gourmet breakfast...make a variety, adding chives, sausage or even broccoli.

1/2 of a 2.8-oz. pkg. cooked
   bacon
9-inch pie crust

2 8-oz. cartons egg substitute
8-oz. jar creamy blue cheese
   salad dressing

Crumble the bacon into the pie crust. Blend together the egg substitute and the salad dressing in a large bowl; pour into pie crust. Bake 25 to 30 minutes at 350 degrees, or until puffed and a knife inserted in the center comes out clean. Cool on a wire rack for 5 minutes before cutting. Makes 4 to 6 servings.

Print holiday sentiments on vellum, using old-fashioned curly fonts for heartfelt wishes. Punch out the message, using circular or square hand-held paper punches, and attach to packages with cotton string.

Good Morning Cheer

Glazed Mincemeat Coffee Ring

Donna Gonda
North Canton, OH

Our daughter was born on Christmas Day in 1950 and our son was born several years later. When they were young, the excitement and anticipation of Christmas and birthday gifts as well as visitors made it difficult to encourage them to eat breakfast. It became our tradition to serve a simple breakfast of this coffee ring with fresh fruit.

2 c. all-purpose flour	3/4 c. prepared mincemeat
3/4 c. sugar	1/2 c. milk
2-1/2 t. baking powder	3/4 c. brown sugar, packed
1/2 t. salt	2 T. water
1/3 c. butter	1 T. corn syrup
1 egg, beaten	1 c. powdered sugar

Combine flour, sugar, baking powder and salt in a large mixing bowl; cut in butter until mixture resembles fine crumbs. In a second mixing bowl, combine egg, mincemeat and milk; add all at once to flour mixture. Stir until just moistened; spread evenly in a greased and floured 6-1/2 cup ring mold. Bake for 25 to 30 minutes at 375 degrees, or until a toothpick inserted near center removes clean. Cool in the pan on a wire rack for 10 minutes; turn out onto serving plate. Combine brown sugar, water and corn syrup in a medium saucepan; heat and stir just to boiling. Remove from heat; blend in powdered sugar and mix to a drizzling consistency. Drizzle over warm coffee ring. Serve warm or cold. Makes 8 to 10 servings.

for you

Need a gift in a flurry? Line a clean, new one-gallon paint can with a tea towel, glue homemade paper snowflakes on the outside and then fill to the rim with homemade cookies. Wrap it all up in cellophane and tie with a homespun bow.

Heat & Hold Scrambled Eggs

Judy Collins
Nashville, TN

Serve with a stack of buttered toast and platter of sausage links.

1/4 c. butter
12 eggs
1-1/3 c. milk
1 t. salt

1/8 t. pepper
2 T. all-purpose flour
1 T. pimento, chopped
1 T. fresh parsley, chopped

Melt butter in skillet over low heat. Combine remaining ingredients in large bowl; beat until smooth and pour into skillet. Heat until eggs are set to desired consistency. Can be held for up to one hour in a chafing dish or electric skillet set at 200 degrees. Serves 6.

Southern-Style Cheese Grits

Tammie Watson
Morris, GA

A warm, hearty breakfast side dish we all enjoy.

2 c. water
1/2 t. salt
1/2 c. quick-cooking grits,
  uncooked

2 eggs, beaten
1/4 c. margarine
1/2 c. milk
1 c. shredded Cheddar cheese

Bring water and salt to a boil; stir in grits. Cook on medium heat for 4 to 5 minutes. Stir in remaining ingredients except cheese; cook for another 4 to 5 minutes. Pour mixture into a greased 8"x8" baking pan; sprinkle with cheese. Bake at 350 degrees for one hour. Serves 4.

Good Morning Cheer

Eggnog French Toast

Joy Davis
Dexter, OR

A sweet, cinnamon twist on an old family favorite.

2 eggs
1/2 c. eggnog
1/8 t. nutmeg

1/8 t. cinnamon
4 slices cinnamon-raisin bread
1 to 2 T. butter

Beat eggs and eggnog together; add nutmeg and cinnamon. Soak bread in mixture until coated; set aside. Melt butter in a skillet; add bread. Heat until bread is golden; flip bread and repeat with the other side. Serves 4.

Christmas waves a magic wand over this world, and behold, everything is softer and more beautiful.

-Norman Vincent Peale

Mexican Hot Chocolate

Jessica Parker
Mulvane, KS

Cinnamon adds a south-of-the-border touch!

6 c. milk, divided
1/2 c. sugar
3 oz. unsweetened chocolate,
   chopped
1 t. cinnamon

2 eggs, beaten
1 T. vanilla
Garnish: whipping cream,
   whipped

Combine one cup milk, sugar, chocolate and cinnamon in a large saucepan; stir over medium-low heat until chocolate is melted. Gradually stir in remaining milk. Heat and stir until milk is very hot; do not boil. Gradually stir one cup hot mixture into eggs, then return entire mixture to saucepan; heat and stir for 2 minutes over low heat. Remove from heat, stir in vanilla, and beat with a beater until very frothy. Pour into mugs and garnish with whipped cream. Makes 6 servings.

Hot glue giant pine cones to lengths of drapery cord and tie into a bundle. Hang on the front door for a merry farmhouse welcome!

Good Morning Cheer

My Favorite Brunch Recipe

Karen Puchnick
Butler, PA

A brunch dish that looks like a quiche, tastes delicious and there's nothing complicated about making it. Try adding favorite toppings...chopped tomatoes, spinach, rosemary or pesto sauce.

2 c. redskin potatoes, cubed
2 T. butter
1 onion, chopped
1/2 c. red or green pepper,
   finely chopped

4 slices cooked ham or bacon,
   cut into 1/2-inch pieces
salt and pepper to taste
3 eggs
2 T. milk

Sauté potatoes in butter in a skillet; when potatoes are golden, add onion and pepper and heat until onion is translucent. Remove from heat and stir in ham or bacon, salt and pepper. Blend together eggs and milk in a small bowl until slightly frothy. Spray a 9" pie plate with non-stick vegetable spray; arrange vegetables and meat evenly in pie plate and pour egg mixture over. Bake at 350 degrees for 12 to 15 minutes, or until eggs are set and a knife comes out clean when inserted in the center. Makes 4 to 6 servings.

Gather paper-crafting supplies and place in a colorful gift bag to drop off to an avid scrapbooker...include some textured papers and 3-D stickers for even more scrapbooking fun.

Raspberry Muffins

Elisabeth Macmillan
British Columbia, Canada

Try blackberries instead of raspberries, or a combination of the two!

2 c. all-purpose flour
1 c. brown sugar, packed
1-1/2 t. baking powder
1 t. baking soda
1/2 t. salt
1 c. quick-cooking oats,
    uncooked

2 eggs
1/3 c. oil
2 t. vanilla extract
1-1/2 c. buttermilk
3 to 4 c. frozen whole
    raspberries

Combine flour, brown sugar, baking powder, baking soda, salt and oats in a large bowl; set aside. Combine eggs, oil, vanilla and buttermilk in a separate bowl; blend well. Pour egg mixture over flour mixture and stir just until dry ingredients are moistened; set aside. Place frozen berries in a large plastic zipping bag, seal and crush using hands or a rolling pin; measure out 2 cups crushed berries. Gently stir berries into flour mixture and spoon into 12 greased or paper-lined muffin cups. Bake at 375 degrees for 20 to 25 minutes. Makes one dozen.

Wrap gifts in fun coordinating papers, ribbons and berry sprigs, then stack and secure with lengths of ribbon. What a delightful way to deliver gifts to friends and family!

Good Morning Cheer

Golden Peach Muffins

Barbara Sherman
Magna, UT

Add a tablespoon or 2 of chopped pecans to the batter before baking...for muffins they'll go nuts over!

1-1/2 c. all-purpose flour
1 c. sugar
3/4 t. salt
1/2 t. baking soda
1/8 t. cinnamon

2 eggs
1/2 c. oil
1/2 t. vanilla extract
15-oz. can sliced peaches,
    drained and finely chopped

Combine flour, sugar, salt, baking soda and cinnamon in a medium bowl; add eggs, oil and vanilla. Stir until moistened; fold in peaches. Fill 16 paper-lined muffin cups 2/3 full; bake at 375 degrees for 25 to 30 minutes until golden. Makes 16.

A pair of vintage skis or rustic snowshoes gathered together with a big plaid bow or long, knitted muffler makes a cozy-cabin outdoor decoration. When highlighted with a spotlight, the scene can be enjoyed all season long.

Apple Ring Coffee Cake

Jodie Blevins
Vandenberg AFB, CA

This cake was a big hit with my husband's Air Force squadron.

3 c. all-purpose flour
1 t. baking soda
1 t. salt
1 t. cinnamon
1 c. chopped walnuts
1-1/2 c. sugar

1 c. oil
2 t. vanilla extract
2 eggs
2 c. tart apples, peeled
   and chopped

Combine flour, baking soda, salt and cinnamon in a large bowl; stir in walnuts and set aside. Combine sugar, oil, vanilla and eggs in a medium bowl; stir in apples, then add to flour mixture and stir just until moistened. Spoon batter evenly into a greased 10" tube pan. Bake for one hour at 325 degrees until a toothpick comes out clean. Cool in pan on wire rack for 10 minutes; remove from pan and return to wire rack to cool completely. Makes 12 servings.

Tuck sprigs of pepperberries & greenery into a shiny new paint can. Wrap in Christmasy homespun and tie on a bow of raffia, for a bright spot of color on your table.

Good Morning Cheer

Christmas Morning Chile Relleno

Angela Leikem
Silverton, OR

*Serve with fruit salad and sausage links for a spicy
Christmas breakfast.*

16-oz. pkg. shredded Cheddar
   cheese
16-oz. pkg. shredded Monterey
   Jack cheese
2 4-oz. cans chopped
   green chiles

4 eggs
1/4 c. all-purpose flour
1 c. evaporated milk

Sprinkle cheese and chiles together alternately in a greased
13"x9" baking pan. Whisk together eggs, flour and milk in a medium
bowl and pour over cheese mixture. Bake at 350 degrees for
30 minutes. Let cool slightly before serving. Makes 8 to 10 servings.

To add a spatterware finish to a painted project, just dip
the bristles of a dry toothbrush into paint. Blot on a
paper towel to remove excess paint, then pull your
thumb across the bristles to spatter the
paint…quick & easy speckles!

Banana-Pecan Waffles

Lynda McCormick
Burkburnett, TX

These make a great morning meal or filling supper.

2 eggs
1-1/2 c. buttermilk
1/3 c. butter, melted
1/2 c. ripe banana, mashed
1 t. vanilla extract
2 c. all-purpose flour
2 T. sugar
1 T. plus 1 t. baking powder

1/4 t. salt
3/4 c. chopped pecans
Garnish: maple syrup, sliced
   bananas, whipped cream,
   whipped butter, cinnamon
   sugar, additional chopped
   pecans

Beat eggs in a medium bowl for one to 1-1/2 minutes; blend in remaining ingredients except pecans just until smooth. Pour about 1/2 cup batter onto preheated waffle iron; sprinkle with pecans and bake as manufacturer directs. Top with your choice of garnishes. Makes about six, 8-inch waffles.

Bundle up a bag of
home-baked cookies
in a holiday apron and
tie with a length of
rick-rack. Fill the apron
pocket with the recipe and
a cookie cutter or two.
The happy baker will be
oh-so pleased.

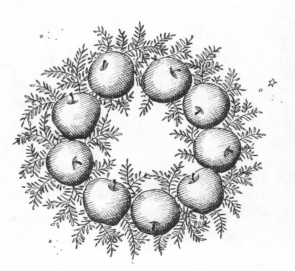

Good Morning Cheer

Cinnamon Pancake Mix in a Jar

Geneva Rogers
Gillette, WY

A thoughtful gift to take along for your hostess when visiting during the holidays.

3 c. all-purpose flour
4 t. cinnamon
2-1/4 T. sugar

2 T. baking powder
1-1/4 t. salt

Layer all ingredients in a one-quart, wide-mouth jar in order given. Attach the following instructions.

Instructions:

Combine 3/4 cup milk, one egg and 2 tablespoons oil in a medium bowl; set aside. Empty jar contents into a second bowl and mix well; measure out 1-1/3 cups, returning rest of mix to jar for future use. Whisk flour mixture into milk mixture until moistened. Heat a lightly oiled griddle over medium-high heat. Pour 1/4 cup batter onto the griddle for each pancake. Heat until golden on both sides.
Makes 5 servings.

Tuck Cinnamon Pancake Mix in a Jar into a basket along with a jug of real maple syrup, a new extra-large spatula and some flavored teabags. Any busy family will enjoy this breakfast treat.

Feather Bed Eggs

Karen Pilcher
Burleson, TX

*Sprinkle bread cups with diced ham, onion, green pepper or
mushrooms for variety before adding the shredded cheese and eggs.*

2 T. butter, softened	6 eggs
6 thick slices bread	1-1/2 c. milk
pepper to taste	oregano to taste
1-1/2 c. shredded Cheddar	
cheese, divided	

Grease 6 large muffin cups. Butter one side of each bread slice, place
buttered-side up in muffin cup and press into place. Sprinkle each slice
of bread with pepper to taste and 1/4 cup cheese. Beat eggs and milk
together in a large bowl and add oregano to taste; divide mixture
among muffin cups. Cover and refrigerate overnight. In the morning,
uncover and bake at 350 degrees for 30 to 40 minutes or until puffed
and golden. Serve hot. Makes 6.

Fill a big wooden dough bowl or sap bucket with
individually-wrapped popcorn balls and set near the front
door. Hand them out as a sweet "glad-you-stopped-by" gift.

Good Morning Cheer

Orange-Pecan Muffins

Mallory Kae
Delaware, OH

"Orange" ya glad you found this yummy muffin recipe?

3 T. butter, softened
1/2 c. sugar
2 egg whites
1/2 c. buttermilk
1/4 c. orange juice
1 t. vanilla extract

1-1/4 c. all-purpose flour
1/2 t. baking soda
1/4 t. salt
1 T. orange zest
1/4 c. chopped pecans

Blend together butter and sugar in a medium bowl; set aside. Combine egg whites, buttermilk, orange juice and vanilla; stir into butter mixture. Combine flour, baking soda and salt and stir into butter mixture just until blended. Gently stir in orange zest and pecans. Spray 12 muffin cups with non-stick vegetable spray; spoon batter into muffin cups, filling 2/3 full. Bake for 15 to 18 minutes at 400 degrees, until tops are golden. Makes one dozen.

Make your own hot cocoa cones! Just fill disposable frosting bags (found in any cake decorating shop) 2/3 full with hot cocoa mix. Add a layer of mini marshmallows, chocolate chips or even crushed candy canes and close with a twist tie. A welcome gift to send to college students.

Mushroom & Egg Bake

Dianne Medwid
Manitoba, Canada

*Extra delicious when topped with a dollop of sour cream
and a sprinkling of chives.*

1/2 lb. sliced mushrooms	1-1/2 c. shredded Gruyere
2 T. butter	cheese, divided
1 t. lemon juice	1 c. whipping cream, divided
1 t. Worcestershire sauce	4 eggs

Sauté mushrooms in butter, lemon juice and Worcestershire sauce; set aside. Sprinkle 3 tablespoons of cheese in the bottom of each of 4 buttered ramekins; pour 1/4 cup cream in each. Break an egg over the top of cream; spoon 1/4 of the mushroom mixture over each egg. Top each with 1/4 of the remaining cheese; set aside. Fill a 13"x9" pan with 3/4-inch water; add ramekins. Cover; bake at 350 degrees for 15 minutes. Uncover; bake for an additional 10 to 15 minutes. Serves 4.

String a garland of kumquats and lady apples to
drape around the front door…such a simple yet
colorful holiday decoration.

Good Morning Cheer

Jelly-Roll Pancakes

Renae Scheiderer
Beallsville, OH

Try pumpkin butter or apple butter instead of jam or jelly!

1 c. all-purpose flour	2 eggs
1-1/2 t. baking powder	3 T. oil
1/2 t. salt	1/3 c. jam or jelly
1 c. milk	Garnish: powdered sugar

Stir together flour, baking powder and salt in a medium bowl; set aside. Blend together milk, eggs and oil in a small bowl; stir into flour mixture until just blended. Heat oil on griddle, pour on 1/2 cup batter for each pancake, and heat until golden on both sides. Spread about 2 teaspoons jam or jelly on one side of each pancake; roll up, place seam-side down on serving plate and sprinkle with powdered sugar. Makes about eight, 6-inch pancakes.

Sugared fruit! Evenly coat fruit with corn syrup and then sprinkle with fine sugar, setting each aside until dry for sweet & sparkly centerpieces.

Braided Coffee Bread

Nancy Molldrem
Eau Claire, WI

I make this coffee bread every Christmas Eve just like my mother did when I was a girl. On Christmas morning the house smells so good of fresh-baked bread.

1-1/2 pkgs. active dry yeast
1/4 c. warm water
3 T. sugar
1/2 c. milk, scalded and cooled
3 c. all-purpose flour, divided
3 eggs, beaten

1/2 t. salt
1/2 c. butter, softened
Garnish: powdered sugar
   frosting, chopped nuts,
   chopped maraschino cherries

Dissolve yeast in water; add sugar. Stir in milk and 1/2 cup flour. Blend with hand mixer until smooth; add eggs, salt and butter and blend again with mixer. Stir in rest of flour and knead until smooth; place in bowl, cover, and chill overnight. Divide into 3 parts and form each into a roll about 18 inches long; braid rolls together and let rise until almost double. Bake about 20 minutes at 375 degrees; let cool and garnish with frosting, nuts and cherries. Makes one loaf.

Silver bells…arrange votives in plain glass votive holders on a silver serving tray. Spiral shiny silver beads between the votives with a scattering of silver jingle bells.

Good Morning Cheer

Country Breakfast Casserole

Hattie Douthit
Crawford, NE

What could be "ch-easier" than this family favorite?

12 slices bread, cubed
2 c. cooked ham, cubed
12 eggs

4 c. milk
salt and pepper to taste
2 c. shredded Cheddar cheese

Layer bread and ham in a greased 13"x9" baking pan; set aside. Blend together eggs, milk, salt and pepper; pour over bread. Sprinkle with cheese; refrigerate overnight. Bake at 350 degrees for one hour. Serves 8 to 10.

Slice canned cranberry sauce into 1/2-inch thick rounds and use a star or heart cookie cutter to cut out shapes. Tuck into fruit cups for a tangy breakfast surprise.

French Toast Casserole

Lee Ann McMath
Uhrichsville, OH

This recipe is a Christmas morning tradition at our house. It is assembled Christmas Eve and popped into the oven when we get up, allowing everyone to enjoy their gifts while breakfast is baking.

1-1/2 lb. loaf French bread,
   sliced 1-inch thick
8 eggs
3 c. milk
4 t. sugar
3/4 t. salt

1 T. vanilla extract
2 t. butter
Optional: cinnamon
Garnish: maple syrup, honey, or
   sliced strawberries

Generously butter a 13"x9" pan or spray with non-stick vegetable spray. Arrange bread slices in a single layer over bottom of pan. Beat eggs, milk, sugar, salt and vanilla together and pour over bread. Dot with butter; sprinkle with cinnamon if desired. Cover and refrigerate overnight. Bake at 350 degrees for 45 minutes, until puffy and golden. Serve with maple syrup, honey or sliced strawberries. Serves 8.

To make a taper candle fit snugly in its holder, wrap a rubber band several times around the bottom of the candle...no need to worry about tipping.

46

Good Morning Cheer

Bacon-Onion Quiche

Corky Adams
Owosso, MI

1-2-3, it's breakfast!

1 lb. bacon, crisply cooked and
   crumbled
1-1/2 c. shredded Swiss cheese
1/2 c. onion, chopped
9-inch pie crust

4 eggs
1/2 c. milk
1-oz. pkg. ranch dressing mix
salt and pepper to taste

Combine bacon, cheese and onion; spoon into pie crust. Set aside. Mix remaining ingredients together; pour into pie crust. Bake at 375 degrees for one hour or until center is set. Makes 4 to 6 servings.

Christmas greenery peeking out of stockings adds good cheer and a fresh fragrance for the holidays.

Can't-Fail Biscuits

Arlene Grimm
Decatur, AL

A really easy biscuit recipe. Tasty when spread with jams or honey.

2 c. self-rising flour   1 c. whipping cream

Mix together flour and whipping cream; roll out on a floured board and cut out biscuits with a round cutter. Place on a greased baking sheet and bake 10 to 12 minutes at 375 degrees. Makes about one dozen.

Make it sparkle, make it shine…wrap the Christmas tree trunk with mini white lights and then hang larger, colored lights on the branches!

Good Morning Cheer

Chocolate Gravy for Biscuits

Kelly Summers
Jefferson, OH

We visit my husband's aunt in Georgia every Christmas season. Biscuits with chocolate gravy is one of my favorite memories. This recipe has been a tradition in my husband's family for at least 4 generations now! The men like it so much that they put the chocolate gravy over everything...eggs, bacon, sausage and pancakes.

3 c. sugar
1/4 c. all-purpose flour
1/4 c. baking cocoa

3 c. milk
1 t. vanilla extract
1 T. margarine

Mix sugar, flour, cocoa and milk in a microwave-safe container. Microwave on high setting for 8 to 10 minutes, until thick and bubbly; stir every 2 to 3 minutes. Remove from microwave; stir in vanilla and margarine. To serve, crumble warm biscuits on plates; top with warm gravy. Makes 8 to 10 servings.

Honey Butter

Darlene Owen
Jetersville, VA

Set out 20 minutes or so before serving for easy spreading.

3/4 c. honey
3/4 c. butter, softened

3/4 c. powdered sugar
1 t. cinnamon

Blend together all ingredients; refrigerate. Makes about 2 cups.

Breakfast Cookies

Pat Habiger
Spearville, KS

*There are presents to unwrap, families to visit, boots to find...these
cookies are a nutritious treat when breakfast is forgotten!*

2/3 c. butter, softened
2/3 c. sugar
1 egg
1 t. vanilla extract
3/4 c. all-purpose flour
1-1/2 c. quick-cooking oats,
    uncooked

1/2 t. salt
1/2 t. baking soda
1 c. shredded Cheddar cheese
2 c. wheat germ
6 slices bacon, crisply cooked
    and crumbled

Cream butter, sugar, egg and vanilla together; add remaining
ingredients. Drop by teaspoonfuls onto ungreased baking sheets; bake
at 350 degrees for 12 to 14 minutes. Remove to a wire rack to cool.
Makes 2 dozen.

A simple greenery garland framed around a doorway can
double as a card holder. Just use mini clothespins to clip
holiday cards across the top and down each side.

Making Spirits Bright

Appetizers

Onion Tartlets

Barbara Bongiorno
Jacksonville, FL

A warm, bite-size treat that's sure to please.

1/2 c. mayonnaise
1/2 c. grated Parmesan cheese
1/2 c. onion, chopped
Optional: 1 clove garlic, minced

1 loaf sliced party bread, pita
   triangles or thin-sliced
   baguettes

Blend together mayonnaise, Parmesan, onion and garlic. Spread on bread and arrange on ungreased baking sheets; bake at 350 degrees 10 minutes or until bubbly. Makes one to 2 dozen.

Christmas Tidbits

Phyllis Peters
Three Rivers, MI

Sprinkle with some red and green pepper flakes for a festive touch.

3 T. butter, melted
1 t. dried, minced onion

10-oz. tube refrigerated biscuits
1/4 c. grated Parmesan cheese

Spread butter in a 9"x9" baking pan and sprinkle with onion. Cut each biscuit into 4 pieces; arrange in dish and sprinkle with Parmesan. Bake at 425 degrees for 15 minutes, until golden. Makes 2-1/2 dozen.

Making Spirits Bright

Polish Sausage Appetizer

Marie Alana Gardner
North Tonawanda, NY

*A family-favorite appetizer...I make a triple batch
every Christmas Eve.*

2 lbs. Polish sausage, sliced
3/4 c. brown sugar, packed

1 onion, diced
1 c. applesauce

Combine all ingredients in a 13"x9" baking pan and bake at
350 degrees for one hour, stirring after 30 minutes. Place in a slow
cooker to keep warm for serving. Makes 8 servings.

Pickle Roll-Ups

Doris Taylor
New Concord, OH

Peter Piper didn't pick enough to keep my friends & family happy!

32-oz. jar dill pickles, drained
8-oz. pkg. cream cheese,
    softened

8-oz. pkg. thin-sliced
    deli-style ham

Blot pickles dry with paper towels and spread with cream cheese.
Wrap ham around pickles, securing with an extra dab of cream cheese
as needed. Cover and refrigerate for several hours; slice in half-inch
pieces with a very sharp knife. Makes 6 to 8 servings.

Tie 2 or 3 sprigs of boxwood and juniper together with a red
satin bow, it adds a touch of cheer when tied to the backs of
kitchen or dining room chairs.

Not-Your-Usual Party Mix

Samantha Starks
Madison, WI

A tasty munchie no one can resist.

17.5-oz. pkg. crispy rice cereal
   squares
6-oz. pkg. goldfish-shaped
   crackers
12-oz. pkg. oyster crackers
10.5-oz. pkg. mini cheese-filled
   sandwich crackers

15-oz. pkg. mini pretzel twists
16-oz. pkg. peanuts
12-oz. bottle butter-flavored
   popcorn oil
1-oz. pkg. ranch-style salad
   dressing mix

Combine cereal, crackers, pretzels and nuts in a large mixing bag.
Combine oil and salad dressing mix in a small bowl; toss with cracker
mixture until evenly coated. Store in an airtight container.
Makes 20 servings.

Use champagne flutes as candleholders…fill flutes with
fresh cranberries to anchor candle tapers snugly in place.

Making Spirits Bright

Christmas Cheddar Wafers

Francie Stutzman
Dalton, OH

Sprinkle with toasted sesame seed or coarse pepper...yum!

8-oz. pkg. shredded sharp
   Cheddar cheese
1 c. all-purpose flour
1/2 c. butter, softened

1/2 t. seasoned salt
1/8 t. cayenne pepper
1/2 c. chopped pecans

Mix all ingredients, then form into a roll; wrap in wax paper and chill. Slice thinly and bake on ungreased baking sheets at 350 degrees for 10 to 12 minutes. Makes 6 dozen.

Slow-Cooker English Cider

Mary Ary
Lexington, KY

*My family doesn't think it's Christmas 'til they have each
had a cup (or 2!) of English Cider!*

1/2 c. brown sugar, packed
1-1/2 qts. cider
1 t. whole allspice

2 cinnamon sticks
2 t. whole cloves
1 orange, sliced and seeded

Combine ingredients in slow cooker. Spices can be placed in a tea strainer if preferred, or added loose. Cover and heat on low setting for 2 to 8 hours. Strain before serving if necessary. Makes 1-1/2 quarts.

Cranberry Meatballs

Doreen Adams
Sacramento, CA

A holiday twist on the grape jelly version!

2 lbs. ground beef
1 t. parsley flakes
2 T. soy sauce
1/2 t. garlic salt
2 T. onion, chopped

1 c. quick-cooking oats,
 uncooked
2 eggs, beaten
1/4 t. pepper
1/3 c. catsup

Mix all ingredients thoroughly. Roll into 2-inch balls; arrange in a shallow baking pan and spoon sauce over the top. Bake at 350 degrees for 40 to 50 minutes. Makes 6 to 8 servings.

Sauce:

16-oz. can jellied cranberry
 sauce
12-oz. bottle chili sauce

1/2 c. brown sugar, packed
1 T. lemon juice

Mix all ingredients together.

Colorful pairs of boots lined up from biggest to littlest,
right inside the doorway, will make visitors smile
as they are welcomed in from the snow.

Making Spirits Bright

Ginger-Orange Drummies

Nancy Wise
Little Rock, AR

Arrange on a platter filled with prepared rice...a pretty presentation with its own side dish!

2 c. all-purpose flour
1 T. seasoned salt
2 t. garlic salt
5 lbs. chicken wings
1/3 c. oil

2 c. orange marmalade
1 c. catsup
1/2 c. soy sauce
1 t. ground ginger

Combine flour, seasoned salt and garlic salt in a large plastic zipping bag. Add chicken wings, a few at a time, and shake to coat. Heat oil in a large skillet and fry wings a few at a time, for 3 to 4 minutes on each side, or until golden and crispy. Drain pan drippings and return all wings to pan. Combine marmalade, catsup, soy sauce and ginger; pour over chicken and stir to coat. Cover and cook over medium-low heat for 10 to 15 minutes or until wings are well coated. Makes about 4 dozen.

A seaside holiday! Show off your favorite shells on a pretty platter, then nestle some vintage ornaments among the shells for an easy centerpiece.

Hot Seafood & Artichoke Dip

Joely Flegler
Edmond, OK

When company is expected, use a can of crabmeat and a can of shrimp, then double the amount of both the cream cheese and artichokes for an appetizer large enough to feed 'em all.

8-oz. pkg. cream cheese, softened
1 c. sour cream
1.4-oz. pkg. vegetable soup mix
6-oz. can crabmeat or shrimp, drained

6-oz. jar marinated artichoke hearts, drained and chopped
1/2 c. red pepper, chopped
Optional: 1/2 t. hot pepper sauce

Blend together all ingredients and spread in a 13"x9" baking pan. Bake for 25 minutes at 375 degrees. Makes 4 cups.

A toybox filled with evergreen boughs, well-loved rag dolls and teddy bears and a wrapped gift greets holiday visitors with old-fashioned charm.

Making Spirits Bright

Pap-Pap's Cheese Ball

Dea Jaber
Severn, MD

My grandfather always made these cheese balls for the holidays. When he passed away, I asked for this recipe to remember him by. My friends & family all beg me to make these for them.

6-oz. pkg. crumbled blue cheese
10-oz. jar sharp pasteurized
   process cheese spread
2 T. onion, grated

1 t. Worcestershire sauce
1/2 t. flavor enhancer
4 8-oz. pkgs. cream cheese
8-oz. pkg. sliced almonds

Mix all ingredients except almonds in a large bowl. Form mixture into 4 large balls; roll in sliced almonds and chill. Makes 4 cheese balls.

A stack of painted boxes and trunks in a corner adds a country touch, plus handy storage for giftwraps, ribbons and trimmings. Pretty and practical!

Mozzarella-Stuffed Mushrooms

Doreen DeRosa
New Castle, PA

Serve with garlic bread sticks and a marinara sauce for dipping.

1-lb. pkg. mushrooms
1/4 c. butter, divided
1/3 c. onion, chopped
1 clove garlic, minced
1/3 c. pepperoni slices, chopped

1/3 c. shredded mozzarella
   cheese
1/2 t. Italian seasoning
1/3 c. seasoned bread crumbs

Clean mushrooms; remove and chop stems. Dip mushroom caps into 2 tablespoons melted butter; arrange on baking pan and set aside. Sauté chopped stems, onion and garlic in remaining 2 tablespoons butter until tender. Remove from heat; stir in pepperoni, cheese, seasoning, and bread crumbs and mix well. Spoon into mushroom caps; bake at 350 degrees for 15 minutes or until hot.
Makes about 2 dozen.

No smooshed bows! Tie lengths of tulle around packages and position bows along the narrow side of the gift instead of top and center…great for stacking presents.

Making Spirits Bright

Bruschetta

Paula Lydzinski
Perkasie, PA

Arrange rounds on a holiday platter and tuck in a sprig or 2 of mint leaves or rosemary for added holiday color.

2 to 3 c. plum tomatoes, diced
2 to 6 cloves garlic, pressed
4 to 5 leaves fresh basil, minced
1/3 c. red onion, minced
1/4 c. fresh Italian parsley,
   minced

1/4 c. extra virgin olive oil
1 t. balsamic vinegar
salt and pepper to taste
1/8 t. Italian seasoning
1 baguette or loaf Italian bread,
   sliced and toasted

Combine all ingredients except bread in a large bowl; refrigerate overnight to develop flavor. Serve at room temperature, spread on toasted rounds of bread. Makes one to 2 dozen.

So a-peeling…draw a design on an orange, lemon or lime using a felt tip marker. Carve along the marked design by removing the outside layer of the peel with a vegetable peeler or a lino tool from a hobby store. Stack several in a bowl or on a cake stand for a fragrant centerpiece.

Christmas Wassail

Jennifer Strehlow
Liberty, MO

My mother-in-law always had this waiting for my husband when he would arrive home from college for the holidays. Even years later, one sip brings back those treasured memories of Christmases at home.

1 qt. water	2 c. strong brewed tea
1-1/2 c. sugar	1 qt. cider
5 cinnamon sticks	6-oz. can frozen orange juice
10 whole cloves	concentrate, thawed
5 thin slices fresh ginger root	2 T. lemon juice

Combine water and sugar in a large saucepan; heat over low heat until sugar is dissolved. Add cinnamon, cloves and ginger and let simmer on low for 2 hours, or turn off heat and set aside overnight. Remove spices with a slotted spoon; add tea, cider, orange juice and lemon juice. Heat and serve warm. Makes 3 quarts.

"Cheers!" Fast and easy beverage charms...wrap a thin strip of quilling paper tightly around a pencil, leaving an inch or two uncurled. Using a gel pen, write on each guest's name. When they receive their drink, simply curl it around the stem of their glass.

Making Spirits Bright

Wintry Mix

Linda Mills
Lusby, MD

The sugar coating adds to the snowy look of this crunchy mix.

1 c. semi-sweet chocolate chips
1/2 c. creamy peanut butter
1/4 c. butter
1 t. vanilla extract

9 c. bite-size crispy cereal
  squares
1-1/2 c. powdered sugar

Combine chocolate chips, peanut butter and butter in a microwave-safe bowl and microwave on high, uncovered, for one minute. Stir; microwave an additional 30 seconds, and stir again until smooth. Blend in vanilla. Place cereal in a large bowl; pour mixture over cereal, stirring until cereal is coated. Pour into large plastic zipping bag, add powdered sugar, and shake until well coated. Store in an airtight container. Makes 10 cups.

Perhaps the best Yuletide decoration is being
wreathed in smiles.

-Unknown

Creamy Bacon Bites

Karrie Middaugh
Salt Lake City, UT

These spiraled goodies won't last long!

8-oz. pkg. cream cheese,
   softened
4 slices bacon, crisply cooked
   and crumbled

2 T. onion, chopped
1/8 t. pepper
8-oz. tube refrigerated crescent
   rolls

Combine cream cheese, bacon, onion and pepper; mix well and set aside. Separate dough into 2 rectangles; press together seams and perforations to seal. Spread cheese mixture on dough and roll up into 2 rolls, starting with long side. Press together seams to seal; cut each roll into 16 slices and place cut-side down on ungreased baking sheet. Bake at 350 degrees for 12 to 15 minutes, or until golden. Makes 2-1/2 dozen.

Need a quick hostess gift? Use a dainty, flea-market find teacup and tuck in a little herb plant. Wrap it up in cellophane and add a jolly note...easy, sweet and long lasting!

Making Spirits Bright

Christmas Olive-Nut Spread

Susan Young
Madison, AL

My grandmother Muriel always made this for family gatherings.
Every time I make it, I think of the warmth of her farmhouse kitchen.
Melba toasts and wheat crackers go well with this spread.

8-oz. pkg. cream cheese,
  softened
1/2 c. mayonnaise
3/4 c. finely chopped pecans

1 c. green olives, finely chopped,
  liquid reserved
Optional: hot pepper sauce to
  taste

Blend cream cheese and mayonnaise; add pecans, olives and
2 tablespoons reserved liquid from olives. Stir until well mixed.
Refrigerate for several hours or overnight. Makes 2 cups.

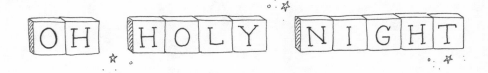

Tory's Favorite Easy Salsa

Linda Quinton
Cumming, GA

Look for red tortilla chips to serve with this holiday salsa!

16-oz. can tomatoes, drained
  and finely chopped
4-oz. can chopped green chiles
1/2 c. onion, finely chopped

1 T. red wine vinegar
1 t. sugar
1/8 t. salt

Mix together all ingredients; let stand 30 minutes at room temperature
before serving. Makes 2 cups.

Working Moms' Cheese Ball

Vickie Garlitz
Edmond, OK

This is easy, quick and tastes great! Use whatever cheeses you have on hand. Dill, garlic, or chive & onion flavored cream cheeses are all tasty. Serve with buttery round or wheat crackers.

2 8-oz. containers flavored
    spreadable cream cheese
1/2 to 1 c. mixed shredded
    cheese

1/2 to 3/4 c. finely chopped
    pecans
Optional: hot pepper sauce to
    taste

Blend cream cheese and shredded cheese in a medium bowl; add pepper sauce, if desired. Form into a ball, roll in chopped pecans; wrap in plastic wrap and refrigerate for an hour before serving. Makes one cheese ball.

Use mini cookie cutters to cut out stars, bells and snowflakes from slices of cheese...add to vegetable trays, tucking in here & there.

Making Spirits Bright

Celebration Punch

Sandi Grock
Huntsville, TX

Make sure to have plastic stemware on hand and encourage the kids to take turns toasting each other with holiday wishes!

2 c. water	1 T. orange zest
1 c. sugar	1 T. lemon zest
24 whole cloves	2-1/2 c. lemon-lime juice
4 cinnamon sticks	2 ltrs. sparkling grape juice
1 whole nutmeg, crushed	Garnish: lemon slices

Heat water in a large pot; add sugar, spices and zests. Bring to boil and heat for 5 minutes; reduce heat and simmer 5 minutes. Strain into a second large pot, add lemon-lime juice and heat until gently bubbling. Add grape juice and keep warm on low heat; garnish with lemon slices. Makes 3 quarts.

Add a bit of sparkle and spice to holiday drinks…tie a little ornament or bauble onto a cinnamon stick. The cinnamon stick is a great stirrer, while the ornament dangles over your mug of hot cocoa, mulled cider or creamy eggnog.

Pepperoni Rolls

Wendy Carl
Red Lion, PA

A filling appetizer for those pizza-loving guests.

24 frozen roll-size dough balls
6 slices mozzarella cheese

8-oz. pkg. pepperoni slices
softened butter

Place dough balls on greased baking sheets to rise as package directs; set aside. Once they have risen, press together in pairs and roll each out, forming 12 ovals. Cut cheese slices in half; arrange one slice on each oval of dough and overlap 6 pepperoni slices on top of each. Tuck in sides of each dough oval, roll up and pinch edges together. Place rolls on greased baking sheets and allow to rise a second time until double. Bake for 15 minutes at 350 degrees till tops are golden. Remove from oven; brush tops with butter. Makes one dozen.

An all-star tree…wrap glittery pipe cleaners around all sizes
of star shapes, twisting ends together to hold the shape.
Make lots of red, white & blue stars for a
patriotic-inspired tree.

Making Spirits Bright

Debbie's Delight

Karen Whitehead
Euless, TX

Your guests won't be able to resist these little treats!

16-oz. pkg. bacon
16-oz. pkg. mini smoked
   sausages

1 c. brown sugar, packed

Cut bacon slices into thirds; wrap each sausage with bacon and fasten with a toothpick. Arrange in a greased baking pan; sprinkle with brown sugar. Bake at 350 degrees for one to 1-1/2 hours, turning occasionally, until bacon is crisp. Makes 12 servings.

Shrimp Butter

Lisa Enoch
Orlando, FL

Fun to serve with fish-shaped crackers!

2 6-oz. cans small shrimp,
   drained
8-oz. pkg. cream cheese,
   softened

1/2 c. butter, softened
4 T. mayonnaise
1 T. lemon juice
1 T. onion, minced

Mix together all ingredients; blend well and chill. Makes 3 cups.

Apple-Cranberry Sparkler

Renae Scheiderer
Beallsville, OH

Looks oh-so pretty when served in tall, sparkling glasses.

4 teabags
2 c. boiling water
1 c. cranberry juice cocktail,
   chilled

1 c. apple juice, chilled
2 t. sugar

Place teabags in boiling water and brew for 5 minutes; remove teabags. Combine tea, juices and sugar in a pitcher and chill. Makes one quart.

May peace and plenty be the first to lift the latch
on your door, And happiness be guided to your home
by the candle of Christmas!

-Irish blessing

Making Spirits Bright

Reindeer Chow in a Jar

MaryAnn Nemecek
Springfield, IL

Even young ones can help with this! Use red and green candy-coated chocolates to make mix especially Christmasy. Pack into pretty jars for gift giving, label as Reindeer Chow and glue a red button on top!

4 c. salted peanuts	1 c. raisins
1 c. whole almonds	1 c. chopped dates
1 c. candy-coated chocolate pieces	1/4 c. shelled sunflower seeds

Combine all ingredients in a large bowl; store in a covered container. Makes 16 servings.

Edible Play Clay

Becky Wilson
Columbus, OH

Preschoolers love this! Shape into animals, beads or whatever they like and when air-dried, it is completely edible.

1/4 c. honey	Garnish: raisins, nuts, coconut,
1/2 c. creamy peanut butter	small candies
1 c. powdered milk, divided	

Mix honey, peanut butter, and 1/2 cup powdered milk using hands or a spoon; keep adding the rest of the powdered milk until dough feels soft, not sticky. Model as you like; garnishes can be pressed in for texture. Allow to dry hard. Makes 1-1/2 cups dough.

Snow Cocoa

Kendall Hale
Lynn, MA

Stir this hot cocoa all together in the slow cooker and plug in before heading out to go sledding.

2 c. whipping cream
6 c. milk
1 t. vanilla extract

12-oz. pkg. white chocolate
chips

Combine all ingredients in a slow cooker. Heat on low for 2 to 2-1/2 hours or until chocolate is melted and mixture is hot. Stir well to blend before serving. Makes 10 servings.

Mocha Cocoa Mix in a Jar

Melody Taynor
Everett, WA

Going skiing? Bring along this mix to enjoy after a day on the slopes!

1-1/2 c. powdered milk
1/2 c. instant coffee granules
1/3 c. brown sugar, packed

2/3 c. mini semi-sweet chocolate
chips

Combine all ingredients and mix well; pack in a one-quart, wide-mouth jar and attach the following instructions. Makes 12 servings.

Instructions:

Combine 2/3 cup boiling water with 1/4 cup mix in a blender; blend until frothy and serve in a mug. Makes 1 serving.

Savor the Season

soups & breads

Savory Beef Stew in a Flash

John Alexander
New Britain, CT

Simply, the aroma of stew says "Home at last!"

1 T. oil
1 lb. boneless beef sirloin steak,
   cut into one-inch cubes
10-3/4 oz. can tomato soup

10-3/4 oz. can onion soup
1 T. Worcestershire sauce
24-oz. pkg. frozen vegetables
   for stew

Heat oil in skillet, add beef and cook until browned and juices evaporate, stirring often. Stir in soups, sauce and vegetables. Heat to a boil, cover and cook over low heat 10 minutes or until meat and vegetables are tender. Makes 4 servings.

Have a ball! Use hot glue to secure dime-store glass ornaments of all kinds to a styrofoam wreath form. Don't forget to first loop a ribbon around the top for hanging.

Savor the Season

Cream Biscuits

Jodi Bielawski
Manchester, NH

Baskets of warm biscuits, bowls of soup and the company of friends will complete any holiday table.

2 c. all-purpose flour
1 T. baking powder
3 T. sugar

1/2 t. salt
1-1/4 c. whipping cream
milk

Combine flour, baking powder, sugar and salt; add cream. Stir mixture until it forms a dough; form into a ball. Knead dough 6 times on a floured surface; roll out 1/3-inch thick on a floured surface. Cut into circles with the rim of a glass; place on an ungreased baking sheet. Brush tops with milk; bake at 425 degrees for 10 to 15 minutes or until golden. Makes one dozen.

Savory Herb Garden Butter

Jennie Gist
Gooseberry Patch

This is a favorite recipe from a long-gone hometown restaurant.

1-lb. pkg. butter, softened
4 t. lemon juice
1/2 t. garlic powder
1 t. dried oregano

1 t. dried chives
1 t. dried thyme
1 t. dried rosemary
1 t. dried tarragon

Blend butter with lemon juice and garlic powder. Crush herbs very fine and stir into butter mixture. Chill overnight. Makes one pound.

Make & Forget Sausage & Veggie Soup

Robin Hill
Rochester, NY

*Just keep adding hearty ingredients to this soup as
the guest list grows!*

14.5-oz. can beef broth
14.5-oz. can Italian stewed
  tomatoes
1-1/2 c. water
10-oz. pkg. frozen mixed
  vegetables

2 c. frozen diced potatoes
8-oz. pkg. smoked sausage,
  sliced
1/4 t. pepper
Garnish: grated Parmesan
  cheese

Combine beef broth, tomatoes with juice and water in a large
saucepan; bring to a boil. Stir in remaining ingredients. Return to
boiling, reduce heat and simmer, covered, for 5 to 10 minutes. Ladle
into soup bowls and sprinkle with Parmesan cheese. Makes
4 servings.

Line up little red enamelware pails filled with sand along
your front steps or sidewalk. Tuck a skinny taper or two
inside each and light...a sparkly entrance for a holiday
open house or Christmas Eve.

Sweet Potato Biscuits

Becca Brasfield
Burns, TN

Spread with rich apple butter or honey for a touch of sweetness.

1-1/2 c. all-purpose flour
1-1/2 c. whole-wheat flour
1/2 t. cinnamon
1/2 t. baking soda
1-1/2 t. salt

1 T. baking powder
1/2 c. butter
15-oz. can sweet potatoes,
    mashed, juice drained &
    reserved

Mix together dry ingredients in a large bowl. Cut in butter, mashed sweet potatoes and 1/2 cup reserved juice until a soft dough forms. Add more juice as needed. Knead and roll out on a floured surface, about 1/2-inch thick. Cut with a 2-3/4 inch biscuit cutter and place on an ungreased baking sheet. Bake for 10 to 12 minutes at 450 degrees. Serve hot. Makes 15 to 16.

Delight family & friends with a snowman soup supper. Using three plates, place the littlest at the top and largest at the bottom of each place setting. Decorate your snowman "face" with cheese cubes, oyster crackers or croutons, use a roll for his tummy and a bowl of soup for his base.

Mexican 2-Bean Chili

Karen Pilcher
Burleson, TX

Chili for the chilly!

1 zucchini, chopped
15-oz. can black beans, drained
   and rinsed
15-oz. can pinto beans, drained
   and rinsed
8.75-oz. can corn, drained
2 14.5-oz. cans chicken broth
16-oz. jar mild thick & chunky
   salsa
8-oz. can tomato sauce

3 c. chicken, cooked and
   shredded
1 clove garlic, minced
1-1/2 to 2 t. chili powder
1 t. dried cumin
Garnish: shredded cheese, sour
   cream, crushed tortilla chips,
   sliced green onions, chopped
   fresh cilantro

Combine all ingredients in a large saucepan. Bring to a boil, reduce heat and simmer 20 minutes. Ladle into bowls and top with garnishes as desired. Makes 6 servings.

Use pearl-headed pins to attach gift tags to wide bands of velvet ribbon wrapped around gift packages...a vintage look for adults only, please!

Savor the Season

Corn Dollar Crisps

Louise McConnell
Reno, NV

My husband is from New Mexico and these little corn dollars are his favorite. We often have these along with a pot of pinto beans and ham hocks on a cold winter night.

1 c. yellow cornmeal	1 t. brown sugar, packed
1/2 t. salt	2/3 c. water
1/4 t. pepper	3 T. butter

Mix cornmeal, salt and pepper in medium bowl; set aside. Combine sugar, water and butter in small saucepan; heat until butter is melted and liquid comes to a rolling boil. Remove from heat; pour into cornmeal mixture and stir well. Use a 1-1/4 inch cookie scoop to place mounds on lightly greased baking sheets. Use a glass to flatten to 1/4-inch thick. Bake at 375 degrees for 20 minutes. Makes 4 to 6.

Sprigs of greenery, tied with a delicate bow and placed along the tops of decorative hanging platters, make a charming wall display for the holidays.

Rich Tomato Bisque

Kathy Grashoff
Fort Wayne, IN

*Make thick grilled cheese sandwiches with French bread slices
to dip in this tomato-filled soup!*

4 T. butter
2 onions, chopped
2 cloves garlic, minced
28-oz. can whole tomatoes
46-oz. can tomato juice

2 bay leaves
8-oz. pkg. cream cheese,
  softened
2 c. half-and-half
salt and pepper to taste

Melt butter in soup pot; add onions and garlic. Cook over medium heat
until onions are soft. Add tomatoes and their juice, tomato juice and
bay leaves; simmer 20 minutes, stirring frequently, breaking up
tomatoes with the side of the spoon. Remove from heat and cool
slightly; remove and discard bay leaves. Purée solids with some of the
liquid in a blender or food processor; blend in the cream cheese. Return
to soup pot; add the half-and-half and salt and pepper to taste. May be
served hot or cold. Makes 6 to 8 servings.

Heap on the wood! The wind is chill;
But let it whistle as it will,
We'll keep our Christmas merry still.

-Sir Walter Scott

Savor the Season

Good Luck Bean Soup in a Jar

Jana Tate
San Antonio, TX

A delightful hostess gift for ringing in the New Year.

2 1-pint clamp-top jars
1/2 c. lima beans
1/2 c. pinto beans
1/2 c. Great Northern beans
1/2 c. red beans

1/2 c. split peas
1/2 c. black-eyed peas
1/2 c. lentils
1/2 c. black beans

In each jar, layer 1/4 cup of each type of bean. Seal lid and attach cooking instructions. Makes 2 jars.

Instructions:

Rinse beans, place in a large bowl, add one to 2 teaspoons salt and cover with water. Let stand overnight. Drain beans, place in a large kettle, add 2 quarts water, one cup chopped ham, and one chopped onion. Simmer for 1-1/2 to 2 hours; add one chopped green pepper and 3 tablespoons lemon juice or one teaspoon lemon pepper. Makes 4 servings.

Stack 2 cake stands together, smallest on top. Cover with lemons, limes, hazelnuts and bundles of fresh rosemary for a 2-tiered, too pretty, too easy centerpiece.

Hearty Beef & Veggie Soup

Beverly Groves
Muncie, IN

*My mother always made this for us. When I had to try it on my own,
I was pleased that it turned out just like hers.*

1/2 lb. ground beef, browned
2 c. carrots, sliced
1 stalk celery, chopped
1 onion, chopped
4-oz. jar sliced mushrooms,
   drained

1/2 c. frozen green peas
1 c. zucchini, chopped
2 8-oz. cans tomato sauce
2 c. beef broth
salt and pepper to taste

Combine all ingredients in a large saucepan, cover and bring to a boil.
Reduce heat and simmer 30 minutes, stirring occasionally. Add salt
and pepper to taste. Serves 8.

Dangle foil-covered cardboard stars from the ceiling
all around the top of the Christmas tree…heavenly!

Savor the Season

Peppery Biscuit Sticks

Virginia Watson
Scranton, PA

Biscuits or bread sticks...these tasty tidbits are great for dipping in soups, stews and sauces.

2 c. all-purpose flour
2 T. sugar
2 t. baking powder
1-1/4 t. pepper, divided
1/4 t. baking soda
1/4 t. garlic powder
6 T. butter, chilled
1/2 c. grated Parmesan cheese
1 egg, beaten
1 c. buttermilk, divided

Combine flour, sugar, baking powder, 1/4 teaspoon pepper, baking soda and garlic powder in a large bowl. Use a fork to cut in butter until mixture resembles coarse crumbs. Stir in cheese. Make a well in the center; set aside. Mix egg and 1/2 cup buttermilk in a small bowl; stir into the flour mixture until just moistened. Turn out dough onto a lightly floured surface; knead just until dough holds together. Pat into a 12"x6" rectangle. Brush lightly with additional buttermilk; sprinkle with remaining pepper and press lightly into dough. Cut into twenty-four, 6-inch long strips. Arrange one inch apart on ungreased baking sheets; bake at 450 degrees 8 minutes or until golden. Makes 2 dozen.

Nostalgic holiday postcards make charming placecards. Punch 2 holes in the top, string with thin velvet ribbon, tie on a pair of jingle bells and loop around dining room chair backs.

Oyster Stew

Sally Kerschen
Dodge City, KS

We make this stew often in the Winter, and we find it just delicious!

2 T. butter
1/2 c. onion, chopped
2 8-oz. cans whole oysters, drained
1 T. flour
2 c. milk
1/2 t. Worcestershire sauce
1/2 T. Cajun fish seasoning
1/2 t. dried parsley
salt and pepper to taste
1 to 2 slices American cheese, chopped

Melt butter in a medium saucepan and sauté onions until transparent. Stir in oysters; when warm, stir in flour to coat onions and oysters. Stir in milk and seasonings; heat until warmed through. Stir in cheese until melted. Makes 2 to 4 servings.

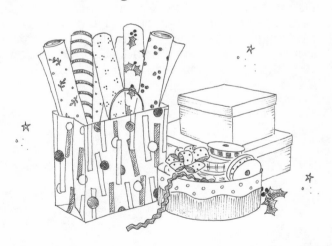

Host a giftwrap party…invite guests to bring their gifts along with rolls of paper to share. Supply tape, tags, tissue paper, cellophane, boxes, bows and other festive trimmings. Play holiday music and serve light refreshments…everyone's gifts will be wrapped in no time at all!

Savor the Season

Dilly Bread

Jeanine Boehm
Pittsburgh, PA

Don't dally, this bread is a must-have!

1 pkg. active dry yeast
1/4 c. warm water
1 c. small-curd cottage cheese
2 T. sugar
1 T. onion, minced
1 T. butter

2 t. dill seed
1 t. salt
1/4 t. baking soda
1 egg
2-1/2 c. all-purpose flour
Garnish: butter, salt

Soften yeast in warm water in a cup. Combine cottage cheese, sugar, onion, butter, dill seed, salt, baking soda, egg and yeast mixture in a large bowl. Add flour one cup at a time to form a stiff dough, mixing well after each addition. Cover bowl; place in warm place and let rise 85 to 90 minutes until dough doubles in bulk. Punch down and let rise an additional 50 to 60 minutes. Place dough in greased 8" round baking pan; let rise another 30 to 40 minutes. Bake for 40 to 45 minutes at 350 degrees. Brush with butter and sprinkle with salt while still warm. Makes one loaf.

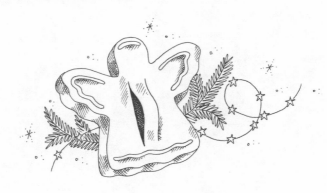

Ho-Ho-Ho! Invite a local Santa to drop in during this year's family get-together. What a joy for all ages!

Sweet Potato Cream Soup

Stephanie Mayer
Portsmouth, VA

Sprinkle with crisp bacon and chopped chives for a tasty addition.

2 c. sweet potatoes, peeled and
    diced in 1/4-inch cubes
1 leek, thinly sliced
14.5-oz. can chicken broth,
    divided
5-oz. can evaporated milk

1-1/2 t. Dijon mustard
1/2 t. salt
1/8 t. white pepper
1/8 t. nutmeg
Garnish: chopped leek

Combine sweet potatoes, leek, and 1/2 cup broth in a 1-1/2 quart
casserole dish; stir well. Cover and microwave on high 5 minutes; stir
and microwave an additional 5 minutes. Pour into a blender; blend
until smooth. Add reserved broth, milk, mustard and seasonings;
blend 30 seconds until smooth. Garnish with chopped leek, if desired.
Serve warm. Makes 4 servings.

What's more cozy than gathering round the fireplace for hot
cocoa and a chat? Stencil pine trees and stars on a large,
galvanized tub to fill with wood and set by the fire to save
trips out into the blustery evening.

Savor the Season

Hazelnut Raisin Cornbread

Robin Carmen
Des Moines, IA

This recipe won a blue ribbon once at the Iowa State Fair!

1 c. golden raisins
1 c. boiling water
2 c. all-purpose flour
14.75-oz. can cream-style corn
1 t. baking soda
1/8 t. salt

1 c. butter
1 c. sugar
2 eggs
1 c. hazelnuts, finely crushed
Garnish: honey, crushed
    hazelnuts

Put raisins into a small bowl; cover with boiling water and let stand 20 minutes. Sift together flour, baking soda and salt. Cream together butter and sugar in a separate bowl; stir in eggs, then flour mixture. Drain raisins and pat dry. Stir raisins, corn and nuts into mixture. Mix well and pour into two, 8"x4" greased and floured loaf pans. Bake for 50 to 60 minutes at 350 degrees until a toothpick removes clean. Turn out of pans; brush with honey and sprinkle crushed hazelnuts on top. Makes 2 loaves.

Clip mini round glass ornaments around the bottom rim of a lampshade…a sparkling touch for the holidays.

Chicken Cacciatore Soup

Kathy Unruh
Fresno, CA

Add a couple drops of hot pepper sauce for those who like it hot!

1 c. rotini pasta, uncooked
3 14.5-oz. cans vegetable
   broth, divided
1/2 lb. boneless, skinless
   chicken breasts, cut into
   bite-size pieces
30-oz. jar extra chunky
   spaghetti sauce with
   mushrooms

14.5-oz. can stewed tomatoes
   in juice, chopped
1 zucchini, sliced
1 onion, chopped
2 cloves garlic, chopped
1/2 t. Italian seasoning
Optional: 1 T. red wine

Cook rotini according to package directions, substituting one can broth for part of the water; set aside. Combine remaining ingredients in a large saucepan. Simmer 20 to 30 minutes, until chicken is cooked through and vegetables are tender. Stir in rotini and heat through. Makes 5 servings.

Joyous wishes…drape a wide, satin ribbon from one end of the mantel to the other. Cut out large letters spelling "Joy to the World" or "Peace on Earth" out of sheet music. Decoupage to letters cut from lightweight cardboard to keep from curling, hang from the ribbon and enjoy!

Savor the Season

Grilled Parmesan Herb Bread

Christine Lennon
Tunkhannock, PA

Use fresh Parmesan cheese and grate right before adding...a little effort that results in a lot of flavor.

1/2 c. butter, softened
1/2 c. grated Parmesan cheese
1 t. dried oregano
1 t. dried parsley

1 t. dried basil
1 loaf Italian bread, sliced
   1-inch thick

Blend together butter, cheese and herbs; spread on both sides of bread slices. Arrange slices on broiler pan and grill until golden.
Makes one loaf.

A tin picnic basket lined with holiday tea towels makes an inviting cookie holder when lots of guests are expected.

Spicy Potato Soup

Jennifer Eveland-Kupp
Reading, PA

One potato, two potato, three potato, four...make this soup and they'll be lining up at the door!

1 lb. ground beef
1 onion, chopped
4 c. potatoes, cubed
3 c. tomato juice
4 c. water

1 to 2 carrots, diced
1 stalk celery, diced
2 T. salt
1-1/2 T. pepper
1/2 t. chili powder

Cook ground beef and onion together in skillet until onions are tender. Stir in remaining ingredients and simmer for one hour.
Makes 16 servings.

Enjoying a cowboy Christmas? Decorate a grapevine wreath with tin stars and dangle a child-size cowboy boot in the center using a big bandanna bow, then hang from the barn door or garden shed!

Savor the Season

Boston Brown Bread

Regina Vining
Warwick, RI

An old-fashioned, hearty bread that's delicious served warm, spread with butter or cream cheese!

1 c. raisins	1-1/2 t. baking soda
1 c. boiling water	1 t. salt
1 c. all-purpose flour	1/4 c. brown sugar, packed
1 c. whole-wheat flour	2 c. buttermilk
1 c. cornmeal	1 c. molasses

Put raisins into a small bowl; cover with boiling water and let stand 15 minutes. Combine dry ingredients in a large mixing bowl; mix well and set aside. Drain raisins and pat dry; combine with buttermilk and molasses. Add buttermilk mixture to flour mixture; stir just until blended. Pour into a greased 9"x5" loaf pan; bake for one hour at 350 minutes. Makes one loaf.

Cranberry-Orange Butter

Linda Grubbs
Rural Hall, NC

Spread on toast, biscuits or croissants...a colorful addition to the holiday table.

1 c. butter, softened	12.75-oz. jar orange marmalade
3-oz. pkg. cream cheese, softened	16-oz. can whole cranberry sauce

Blend together butter, cream cheese and marmalade until creamy; stir in cranberry sauce until well blended. Store in refrigerator. Makes 4 to 5 cups.

Corn & Smoked Sausage Chowder

Denise Van Verth
Sharon, PA

*This is one of my husband's favorite recipes when served
with a salad and fresh-baked bread.*

4 T. butter
2 T. all-purpose flour
1-lb. pkg. smoked sausage, cut
  in 1/2-inch slices, then
  halved
1 qt. milk

16-oz. can cream-style corn
10-3/4 oz. can cream of potato
  soup
1 T. hot pepper sauce
1 T. Cajun seasoning
2 c. shredded Cheddar cheese

Melt butter in a large pot; stir in flour and blend thoroughly. Add
sausage and cook over medium heat for 5 minutes. Add remaining
ingredients, cover and cook over low heat for 40 minutes, stirring
occasionally. Makes 6 servings.

Brown bag it! Crinkle brown paper lunch bags and roll down
the tops. Fill bags with assorted nuts and snacks…quick,
easy and no clean-up!.

Savor the Season

Sourdough Bread Melt

Robin Lind
Pickerington, OH

A fun bread to set in the middle of the table with instructions to just "dig in!"

1-lb. round loaf sourdough
   bread
1-lb. pkg. sliced Monterey Jack
   cheese

1/2 c. butter, melted
Optional: 1/2 c. chopped green
   onions, 1/2 c. chopped green
   chiles

Cut the loaf crosswise without cutting through the bottom crust. Insert cheese slices between cuts. Combine butter, onions and chiles, if using; sprinkle over loaf. Wrap in aluminum foil; place on an ungreased baking sheet and bake for 15 minutes at 350 degrees. Unwrap and bake an additional 10 minutes until cheese is melted. Serve warm. Makes 6 to 8 servings.

Beginning knitter? Scarves are a great first project! Knit a long scarf for each teen on your list...use school colors for a gift that's sure to be a hit!

Banana Bread

Flo Snodderly
North Vernon, IN

Just can't decide whether it's the aroma of baking
or the taste we like best!

1/3 c. oil
1-1/2 c. bananas, mashed
3 eggs

2-1/3 c. biscuit baking mix
1 c. sugar
1/2 t. vanilla extract

Combine all ingredients in mixing bowl; beat with spoon 30 seconds.
Pour into a greased 9"x5" loaf pan and bake at 350 degrees 50 to
60 minutes or until a toothpick inserted in center comes out clean.
Cool 5 minutes before removing from pan. Makes one loaf.

Peach Butter

Tina Wright
Atlanta, GA

A quick and tasty spread to sweeten any meal.

1/2 c. butter, softened

1/4 c. peach jam

Blend together butter and jam until smooth. Makes 3/4 cup.

Pack homemade fruit butter in
an old-fashioned canning jar.
Tie on a mini ladle along with a
handwritten note…a gift full
of sweet holiday wishes!

Savor the Season

Pineapple-Zucchini Bread

Shelly Buckley-Durst
Knoxville, TN

Make 'em by the dozen, wrap each in a brand new tea towel and deliver to neighbors along with a wish for a healthy holiday!

20-oz. can crushed pineapple, drained
1 c. oil
2 c. sugar
2 c. zucchini, grated
3 eggs
2 t. vanilla extract

3 c. all-purpose flour
2 t. cinnamon
1 t. nutmeg
1/2 t. baking powder
1 t. baking soda
1 t. salt

Combine first 6 ingredients; mix in remaining ingredients and pour into 2 greased 9"x5" loaf pans. Bake at 325 degrees for one to 1-1/2 hours or until a toothpick tests clean. Makes 2 loaves.

I wish we could put up some of the Christmas spirit in jars
and open a jar of it every month.

-Harlan Miller

Velvet Pumpkin Bread

Toni LePrevost
Parma, OH

This makes the best quick bread...sifting is the secret.

3 c. all-purpose flour
1 t. salt
2 t. baking soda
2 t. baking powder
2 t. cinnamon

1-1/2 c. oil
2 c. sugar
4 eggs, well beaten
2 c. canned pumpkin

Sift together flour, salt, baking soda, baking powder and cinnamon three times; set aside. Combine oil and sugar in a second bowl and mix well; blend flour mixture into oil mixture. Add eggs and pumpkin; mix well. Pour into 2 greased 9"x5" loaf pans; bake for one hour at 350 degrees. Makes 2 loaves.

No tree necessary...tie brightly colored ornaments in
all shapes & sizes with fishing line and hang in doorways,
windows or simply from the ceiling!

Savor the Season

Cranberry Pecan Loaf

Dianna Likens
Gooseberry Patch

So nice to have on hand when friends & family
stop by for a quick visit.

2 c. all-purpose flour
2 t. baking powder
1 t. salt
1 c. butter, softened
1 c. sugar
3 eggs

2 t. vanilla extract
2/3 c. milk
1-1/2 c. cranberries
1 c. pecans, coarsely chopped
1 c. flaked coconut

Combine flour, baking powder and salt in a mixing bowl; set aside.
Combine butter, sugar, eggs and vanilla in a large mixing bowl; use a
hand mixer at low speed to mix together well. Add flour mixture in
3 additions alternately with the milk, mixing just to blend after each
addition. Stir in cranberries, pecans and coconut; spread in 2 greased
8"x4" loaf pans. Bake for one hour and 25 minutes at 350 degrees.
Cool completely in pans on wire rack. Makes 2 loaves.

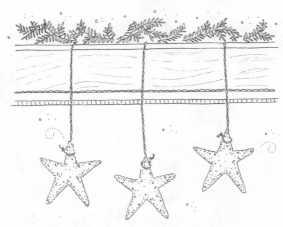

Christmas by the seashore...remind everyone of summer's
favorite vacation spot by tying starfish with jute and
hanging in a row from a bookshelf or mantel.

Black Walnut Bread

Tina Goodpasture
Meadowview, VA

Drizzle with melted chocolate before slicing for an extra-sweet treat.

3 c. self-rising flour
1-1/2 c. sugar
1-1/2 c. milk
3/4 c. butter, softened
1 t. vanilla extract

2 eggs
1-1/2 c. chopped black walnuts,
　divided
Garnish: honey

Mix flour and sugar in a medium bowl; add milk, butter, vanilla extract and eggs and mix well. Add 1-1/4 cups walnuts. Pour into greased, floured 9"x5" loaf pan. Bake for one hour at 350 degrees. Cool for 15 minutes; spread honey on top of loaf and sprinkle with remaining walnuts. Makes one loaf.

Even the littlest elves will enjoy snipping designs out of old Christmas cards. Once they're cut, glue onto store-bought or handmade gift tags that add charm to every package!

Yummy Sides Awaiting

sides & salads

Sweet Potato Crunch

Stacy Wildman
Urbana, OH

*Sprinkle the top with mini marshmallows and place under the broiler
until melted and golden for an extra-special treat.*

4 sweet potatoes, peeled, boiled
   and mashed
3 eggs
1 c. sugar
1 c. margarine, melted and
   divided

1/2 c. milk
2 t. vanilla extract
1 c. brown sugar, packed
1/2 c. all-purpose flour
1 c. chopped pecans

Combine sweet potatoes, eggs, sugar, 1/2 cup margarine, milk and
vanilla; mix well. Pour into a 2-quart casserole dish; set aside. Mix
brown sugar, flour, pecans and remaining margarine together; sprinkle
on sweet potato mixture. Bake at 350 degrees for one hour.
Makes 4 to 6 servings.

Go nutty! Place nuts one-by-one in a small
c-clamp, drill a hole through each using a 1/8" drill bit, then
string onto 22-gauge wire. Make garlands as long as you like,
to hang from a stair railing or mantel!

Yummy Sides Awaiting

Golden Onions

Marie Warner
Jennings, FL

A warm, tasty side that goes especially well with beef roasts.

3/4 c. butter, melted and divided
6 onions, sliced
10-3/4 oz. can cream of chicken
   soup
1 c. milk

1/4 t. salt
1/4 t. pepper
3 c. shredded Swiss cheese
6 slices bread

Combine 1/2 cup butter and onions in a large skillet; heat and stir frequently for 15 minutes or until tender. Pour into a greased 2-quart baking pan; set aside. Combine soup, milk, salt and pepper; spoon over onions and set aside. Brush the remaining butter over bread slices; arrange on top of onion mixture. Bake at 350 degrees for 25 to 30 minutes or until golden. Serves 6 to 8.

How "novel"…stand 2 open vintage books on end, tie into the square formed with jute, place a vase filled with flowers and pine boughs in the center. A sweet way to display treasured childhood Christmas storybooks.

Grampie's Thanksgiving Dressing

Lisa Ludwig
Fort Wayne, IN

Using a slow cooker frees up the oven for that tasty turkey or scrumptious pumpkin pies!

1/2 c. onion, chopped
1/2 c. celery, chopped
2 c. chicken broth
12 to 15 slices bread, toasted
and cubed

1 egg, beaten
1 t. dried basil
1/2 t. dried sage

Simmer onion and celery in broth until tender; cool. Toss remaining ingredients in a large bowl; slowly add cooled broth and mix lightly. Spoon into lightly greased slow cooker; heat on low setting for 3 to 4 hours. Makes 6 to 8 servings.

Warm and welcoming! Light the path with luminarias...fill lunch bags or canning jars about 1/3 full with sand, then nestle a votive in each. Light just in time to greet your first guests.

Yummy Sides Awaiting

Fresh Cranberry Relish

Karen Healey
Rutland, MA

I make this simple recipe every Thanksgiving and Christmas at the request of my dad and husband. It nicely complements all the holiday favorites...turkey, ham, pork roast and stuffed winter squash. I like to garnish it with stars cut from the orange peel with a small cookie cutter.

12-oz. pkg. cranberries
2 apples, cored, peeled and
    quartered
2 pears, cored, peeled and
    quartered

2 oranges, peeled and sectioned
Optional: 1/2 c. coarsely
    chopped pecans
orange zest to taste
honey to taste

Coarsely chop the fruit with a food processor. Mix in nuts and orange zest; sweeten to taste with honey. Turn into a serving dish. Makes about 8 cups.

Sing hey! Sing hey! For Christmas Day
Twine mistletoe and holly
For friendship glows in winter snows
And so let's all be jolly.

-Old Christmas Greeting

Italian Green Beans

Sharon Crider
St. Robert, MO

These green beans are delicious...a family favorite.

10-oz. pkg. frozen green beans
3 cloves garlic, peeled
1/2 t. salt
1/8 t. pepper

1/4 c. red wine vinegar
2 T. olive oil
Garnish: 2 eggs, hard-boiled,
   peeled and sliced

Prepare beans according to package directions; drain. In a small bowl, mash garlic thoroughly with salt, pepper, vinegar and oil. Pour mixture over beans; cover and let stand for one hour. Just before serving, warm over low heat. Turn into serving dish; garnish with eggs. Makes 4 to 6 servings.

Make-Ahead Mashed Potatoes

Karen Antonides
Gahanna, OH

A time-saving recipe so the cook can enjoy her family and guests, too.

5 lbs. potatoes, peeled,
   quartered and boiled
3-oz. pkg. cream cheese,
   softened

2 c. sour cream
1 T. butter, softened
salt, pepper and paprika to taste

Mash potatoes in a large bowl; blend in cream cheese, sour cream and butter. Add salt, pepper and paprika to taste. Spread in a greased 13"x9" baking pan; cover and refrigerate overnight. Bake, covered, for 30 minutes at 350 degrees. Serves 8 to 10.

Yummy Sides Awaiting

Lime Coleslaw Salad

Jo Ann Belovitch
Stratford, CT

A tasty, holiday gelatin salad.

6-oz. pkg. lime gelatin mix
2 c. boiling water
1 pt. lime sherbet, softened

2 c. cabbage, shredded
Garnish: sour cream

Dissolve gelatin mix in boiling water, add sherbet and stir until melted. Stir in cabbage. Pour into an 8"x8" square baking pan or a gelatin mold. Cover and chill about 4 hours, until set. Cut into squares; garnish with sour cream. Makes 8 to 10 servings.

Paper snowflakes cut from newspapers, brown paper bags or vintage maps turn a kid's room into a blizzard of holiday fun.

The Best Salad

Taylor Driscoll
Beaver Crossing, NE

This recipe has been served by my husband's family at Thanksgiving and Christmas since the 1960's. We use wheat, sourdough or whatever bread is on hand to make the croutons...much better than store bought!

3 to 4 slices day-old bread,
   crusts trimmed
1-lb. pkg. bacon, crisply cooked
   and crumbled, drippings
   reserved
1/3 c. vinegar
1/3 c. sugar

3 egg yolks
8-oz. container sour cream
1 to 2 T. butter
seasonings or herbs to taste
1 head romaine lettuce, torn into
   bite-size pieces
4 to 5 green onions, chopped

Cut bread into cubes; set aside. Heat 2 tablespoons reserved bacon drippings in skillet; stir vinegar and sugar together and add to skillet. Boil and let reduce for about 5 minutes. Blend together egg yolks and sour cream in a small bowl. Add to skillet, stirring constantly, and allow to cook down about 7 minutes over medium heat until mixture thickens. Melt butter in a saucepan and add seasonings to taste; toss bread cubes to coat. Spread bread cubes on a large baking sheet and bake 10 to 15 minutes at 350 degrees until golden. Arrange lettuce in large salad bowl; pour hot dressing over top. Sprinkle with crumbled bacon, croutons and green onions. Toss before serving. Makes 4 servings.

Yummy Sides Awaiting

Broccoli-Cheese Casserole

Bobbi Carney
Centennial, CO

Add some crunch...sprinkle with French-fried onions before baking.

1 c. celery, chopped
1 onion, chopped
1/4 c. butter
1-1/2 c. prepared rice
10-oz. pkg. frozen chopped
  broccoli, thawed

8-oz. can sliced water chestnuts,
  drained
10-3/4 oz. can cream of
  mushroom soup
8-oz. jar pasteurized process
  cheese sauce

In a medium saucepan, sauté celery and onion in butter. Stir in rice, broccoli, chestnuts, soup and cheese; spread in a 13"x9" baking pan. Bake at 350 degrees for 45 minutes. Serves 8 to 10.

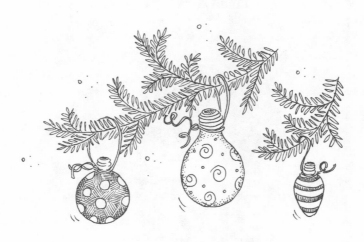

Razzle, dazzle and recycle...paint burned-out light bulbs
of all shapes with glass paint and add swirls or polka dots
with a paint pen. Twist florist's wire around the bases,
leaving an end to shape into a loop for hanging.

Potato Casserole

Nancy Molldrem
Eau Claire, WI

While we were stationed in England with the US Air Force, we became good friends with another young couple who also had a baby. We often shared meals in each other's homes and their friendship became special to us. This potato dish recipe is one that was served by my friend, Barbara, in England.

4 to 6 potatoes, peeled, boiled
   and drained
1-1/2 c. cottage cheese
1/3 c. sour cream

2 T. onion, chopped
salt and pepper to taste
2 T. butter
Garnish: slivered almonds

Mash potatoes in a large bowl; mix with cottage cheese, sour cream, onion, salt and pepper. Spread in a 1-1/2 quart baking pan. Dot with butter, then sprinkle with almonds. Bake at 350 degrees for 30 minutes. Makes 4 to 6 servings.

Have an artificial wreath that's become a bit tattered?
Spray paint it all white. The textures will pop out and
a whole new wreath will emerge.

Yummy Sides Awaiting

Frosty Strawberry Squares

Shirley Gist
Zanesville, OH

This is good as either a dessert or a sweet side dish.

1 c. all-purpose flour
1/4 c. brown sugar, packed
1/2 c. chopped walnuts
1/2 c. butter, melted
2 egg whites
2/3 c. sugar

2 T. lemon juice
10-oz. pkg. frozen strawberries, thawed
1 c. whipping cream, whipped
Optional: whole strawberries

Mix together flour, brown sugar, walnuts and butter. Pat 2/3 of mixture into 13"x9" pan, reserving remaining crumbs. Bake at 350 degrees for 20 minutes, stirring occasionally; remove from oven and set aside. Combine egg whites, sugar, lemon juice and strawberries in a large bowl; blend with hand mixer on high until stiff peaks are formed, about 10 minutes. Fold in whipped cream; spoon over crumb crust. Top with reserved crumbs; freeze for 6 hours or overnight. Cut into squares for serving; if desired, garnish with whole strawberries. Makes 16 servings.

Planning on a new birdbath for this Spring? Buy it now and fill the bowl with an assortment of bulbs. Cover with a round glass table top for an extra end table.

Roasted Cauliflower

Karen Puchnick
Butler, PA

A tasty substitute for deep-fried cauliflower!

2 heads cauliflower, cut into
   flowerets
2 red onions, quartered
1/4 c. olive oil

1/4 t. garlic powder
1/2 t. salt
1/4 t. pepper

Toss cauliflower with other ingredients in a large bowl; spread evenly in a large roasting pan. Cover and bake at 425 degrees, stirring occasionally, 30 to 35 minutes until golden. Makes 8 to 10 servings.

Have a box full of extra buttons? Hot glue to a wreath form for a fun wreath. Try using different shades of all red, green or white for an even more eye-catching design.

Yummy Sides Awaiting

Sweet & Sour Cucumbers

Sharon Crider
St. Robert, MO

A tangy dish that makes a refreshing side!

2 c. cucumbers, peeled and
  thinly sliced
1/2 t. salt
1 c. onions, thinly sliced
1/4 c. vinegar
1 T. water

1 T. sugar
1/2 t. dill weed
1/4 t. pepper
1/8 t. cayenne pepper

Place cucumber slices in a bowl; sprinkle with salt and add cold water
to cover. Refrigerate 30 minutes, then drain well; add onions. Combine
remaining ingredients; pour over cucumbers and onions and toss
lightly. Chill one hour or longer, tossing occasionally, before serving.
Serves 4 to 6.

Make time to stop in and visit at a retirement home.
Just chatting with the residents in the front room will
brighten their day, but most certainly yours also.

Kansas Scalloped Corn

Lori Hobscheidt
Washington, IA

Swiss cheese makes this scalloped corn just a bit yummier!

2 eggs, slightly beaten
11-oz. can corn, drained, liquid
    reserved
14-3/4 oz. can cream-style corn
5-oz. can evaporated milk
4 T. butter, melted

2 T. dried, minced onion
1/8 t. salt
1/8 t. pepper
2 c. saltine crackers, coarsely
    crushed
8-oz. pkg. Swiss cheese, diced

Combine eggs, corn and 1/2 cup reserved corn liquid in a large bowl; add cream-style corn, milk, butter, onion, salt and pepper. Lightly stir in saltines and cheese. Spray an 8"x8" casserole dish with non-stick vegetable spray. Pour in mixture and bake, covered, at 350 degrees for 50 minutes. Uncover and bake an additional 10 minutes until set. Let stand for 5 minutes before serving. Makes 8 to 10 servings.

String seed beads on
12" lengths of florist's wire;
twist the ends to secure
beads in place. Curl around
an empty paper towel tube,
slide off the tube and
voilá…a sparkly napkin
ring in minutes!

Yummy Sides Awaiting

Heather's Awesome Salad

Heather Webb
Richmond, VA

Buy packages of mixed greens and toss this salad together in no time.

2 T. sherry vinegar
2 t. honey
1 t. Worcestershire sauce
1 clove garlic, minced
1/4 c. oil

8 c. mixed greens, torn into
    bite-size pieces
4-oz. pkg. crumbled Gorgonzola
    cheese
3 T. pine nuts, toasted

Combine first 5 ingredients in a large serving bowl; whisk until well blended. Add greens and toss to coat. Sprinkle with cheese and nuts. Serves 8.

Tie sprigs of fresh lavender, thyme and mint together with
a bow to give to friends after a long day of shopping.
Tell them to tie it to the bath faucet and just let the hot
water splash right over the sprigs for a relaxing soak.

Apple Coleslaw

Kathy McLaren
Visalia, CA

Heat up Kielbasa, a package of pierogies and serve with this salad...a warm and filling dinner for a busy evening.

2 c. cabbage, finely shredded
1 tart red apple, cored and
    chopped

1/4 c. poppy seed salad dressing
2 T. sour cream

Toss together cabbage and apple. Combine dressing and sour cream; mix well and toss lightly with cabbage mixture. Chill. Serves 4.

Apple-Onion Sauté

Delinda Blakney
Dallas, GA

To add a bit of color, leave the apples unpeeled.

1/4 c. margarine
1 onion, sliced
 5 Red Delicious apples, cored,
    peeled and sliced
1/2 t. dried basil

1 T. brown sugar, packed
1/4 t. salt
1/2 c. cold water
2 t. cornstarch
1 T. red wine vinegar

Melt margarine in a skillet; add onion and sauté until soft and golden. Stir in remaining ingredients; heat for 5 minutes or until mixture thickens. Serves 4 to 6.

Yummy Sides Awaiting

Squash Puff

Catherine Kellogg
Orlando, FL

Mandarin oranges make this a unique side.

2 10-oz. pkgs. frozen cooked
   winter squash, thawed
1/2 c. brown sugar, packed
1/3 c. butter, melted
1 t. salt
1/2 t. cinnamon
1/2 t. nutmeg

1 egg, beaten
1/2 c. light cream
1/2 c. mandarin oranges
1-1/2 c. mini marshmallows
1/4 c. finely chopped pecans
1/3 c. honey

Mix together the first 9 ingredients; pour into a 3-quart casserole dish. Bake for 25 minutes at 375 degrees. Remove from oven, sprinkle with marshmallows and pecans, and drizzle with honey. Return to oven for an additional 10 minutes. Makes 6 to 8 servings.

A row of red apples tucked into pine boughs
arranged down the middle of the kitchen table offers
guests a simple, country welcome.

"Must-Have Recipe" Salad

Holly Peters
Lino Lakes, MN

A light, fruity salad that looks so pretty in a sparkling glass bowl.

2 5-oz. pkgs. romaine lettuce
1 c. shredded Swiss cheese
1/4 c. sweetened, dried
   cranberries

1 c. cashews
1 apple, peeled and diced
1 pear, peeled and diced

Combine all ingredients in a large serving bowl; toss to mix. Pour salad dressing over salad and toss. Serves 8 to10.

Dressing:

1/2 c. sugar
1/3 c. lemon juice
2 t. red onion, finely chopped
1 t. salt

2/3 c. oil
1 T. poppy seed

Combine sugar, lemon juice, onion and salt in blender container; cover and blend well. While blender is running, add oil in a slow, steady stream; blend until thick and smooth. Add poppy seed and blend an additional 10 seconds to mix.

Yummy Sides Awaiting

Mushroom & Orzo Casserole

Laurie Gross
Thousand Oaks, CA

An easy-to-make side with lots of spicy goodness.

8-oz. pkg. orzo pasta, prepared
1/2 c. margarine, softened
1-1/2 oz. pkg. onion soup mix

4-oz. can mushroom stems and
   pieces, drained

Combine orzo, margarine, soup mix and mushrooms. Pour into a
2-quart casserole dish, cover and bake at 375 degrees for 30 minutes.
Uncover and bake an additional 10 minutes. Serves 6.

Candy canes hooked over picture frames add a
festive holiday note to any room.

Cornbread Stuffing

Kathy Grashoff
Fort Wayne, IN

Mound stuffing on a large platter and top with a baked turkey breast…add teaspoonfuls of cranberry sauce evenly spaced around the rim for a meal that's pretty and filling.

16-oz. pkg. cornbread stuffing
   mix
3 c. water
1/2 c. butter, divided
1 c. onion, chopped

1 c. celery, chopped
1 c. ground Italian sausage,
   browned and crumbled
1 c. sweetened, dried cranberries
1/2 c. chopped pecans

Prepare stuffing according to package directions using 3 cups water and 1/4 cup butter; set aside. Sauté the onion and celery in remaining butter until translucent. Stir onion, celery, sausage, cranberries and pecans into stuffing; toss well to coat. Spread in a lightly greased 13"x9" baking pan; bake at 350 degrees for 30 minutes. Makes about 12 cups.

Write "Welcome One & All!" on a big, black chalkboard and hang on the front door for a festive greeting…a tartan plaid bow makes the ideal hanger.

Yummy Sides Awaiting

3-Cheese Potatoes

Karen Pilcher
Burleson, TX

An all-time favorite year 'round.

1/2 c. butter, melted
2 lbs. potatoes, peeled,
    quartered and boiled
2 t. garlic, minced
4 T. grated Romano cheese,
    divided
1/2 c. milk
1-1/2 c. shredded Monterey Jack
    cheese

1-1/2 c. shredded Cheddar
    cheese
2 T. green onions, chopped
2 t. salt
1 t. pepper
1-1/2 t. white pepper
1 t. paprika

Pour butter over potatoes; add garlic, 3 tablespoons Romano cheese and remaining ingredients. Mix well and spread in a lightly greased 13"x9" baking pan. Sprinkle remaining Romano cheese over top; bake at 350 degrees for 35 minutes. Serves 8.

At Christmas play and make good cheer,
For Christmas comes but once a year.

-Thomas Tusser

Grandma's Poppy Seed Dressing

Kimberly Rockett
Fort Wayne, IN

Grandma was sure to have an empty salad bowl when
she served Poppy Seed Dressing.

3/4 c. sugar
1/2 c. vinegar
1 t. salt
4 T. poppy seed

1 T. dry mustard
1 T. onion, grated
1 c. oil

Blend all ingredients and refrigerate. Shake well before using. Makes 2 cups.

Garlic Vinaigrette

Kathy McLaren
Visalia, CA

A recipe shared from Norway and enjoyed by all.

1-1/4 c. oil
1/2 c. wine vinegar
2 T. sugar

2 T. salt
1/4 t. pepper
6 cloves garlic, pressed

Blend together all ingredients and refrigerate. Stir or shake well before using. Makes 1-3/4 cups.

Visions of sugarplums! Treat the kids (or yourself) on
Christmas Eve to a sweet sampling of Christmas cookies
along with a frothy cup of cocoa
before bedtime...sure to bring
sweet dreams.

Season's Eatin's

Savory Main Dishes

Easiest-Ever Turkey Dinner

Claire Bertram
Lexington, KY

What a wonderful dinner for a small gathering...it can even cook while you're catching up and sharing laughs with your holiday company.

3 potatoes, peeled and cubed
3 skinless turkey thighs
12-oz. jar homestyle turkey
   gravy

1 t. dried parsley
1/2 t. dried thyme
1/8 t. pepper

Arrange potatoes in a slow cooker; place turkey on top. Stir together gravy and seasonings; pour over turkey. Cover and cook on low setting 8 to 10 hours or until juice of turkey is no longer pink when centers of thickest pieces are pierced. Remove turkey and potatoes from slow cooker, using a slotted spoon. Stir gravy and serve with turkey. Makes 6 servings.

Hang colorful tassels from window latches...pretty and oh-so-easy!

✫ Season's Eatin's ✫

Chicken Pot Pie

Maxine Blakely
Seneca, SC

Such a versatile recipe, use canned beef, tuna or even salmon in place of chicken and add any favorite veggies. Leftovers are just as good the next day...but there usually aren't any at my house!

2 c. chicken, cooked and cut into
    bite-size pieces
10-3/4 oz. can cream of chicken
    soup

15-oz. can mixed vegetables,
    drained
2 9-inch pie crusts

Mix chicken, soup and vegetables in a large bowl. Line a 9" pie plate with one crust; pour chicken mixture into crust. Top with second crust, fold edges under and crimp to seal. Cut 4 slits in crust to vent. Bake for 25 to 30 minutes at 425 degrees, until pastry is golden and filling is hot. Makes 4 to 6 servings.

The best of all gifts around any Christmas tree: the presence of a happy family all wrapped up in each other.

-Burton Hillis

Oven-Roasted Ribs

Art Berkowitz
Los Angeles, CA

An easy, delicious dinner when served with potatoes or rice.

1 c. peach preserves
1/4 c. lemon juice
1/4 c. Dijon mustard

4 lbs. beef or pork ribs
salt and pepper to taste

Combine preserves, lemon juice and mustard; mix well. Arrange ribs in a large roasting pan sprayed with non-stick vegetable spray. Add salt and pepper to taste; spread sauce on top. Bake at 350 degrees for one hour or until tender. Makes 6 to 8 servings.

Oven Meatballs

Kathryn Moberg
Saline, MI

Serve with pasta, crusty bread and a salad...yum!

1 lb. ground beef
1 c. Italian bread crumbs
1 onion, minced
1 egg, beaten
2 cloves garlic, minced

10-oz. pkg. frozen chopped
  spinach, thawed and drained
1 t. salt
1 t. pepper
1 t. basil

Mix all ingredients together; shape into sixteen 2-inch balls. Place in a greased 13"x9" baking pan; bake at 400 degrees for 25 minutes. Makes 4 servings.

⭐ Season's Eatin's ☆

Oven-Fried Sesame Chicken

Patrice Nelson
Union City, OH

Steamed broccoli and fried rice round out this meal!

2 T. soy sauce
4 boneless, skinless chicken
   breasts
3 T. sesame seed

2 T. all-purpose flour
1/4 t. salt
1/4 t. pepper
1 T. margarine, melted

Place soy sauce in a shallow dish; add chicken, turning to coat, and set aside. Combine sesame seed, flour, salt and pepper in a large heavy-duty plastic zipping bag. Add chicken; seal bag and shake to coat. Arrange chicken in a 13"x9" baking pan sprayed with non-stick vegetable spray. Drizzle margarine over chicken; bake at 400 degrees for 40 minutes or until chicken juices run clear when cut at thickest part. Serves 4.

Out with the bow, in with the Ho-Ho-Ho! Wrap 3 lengths of ribbon around a package, tying and trimming the ends to the box on the back side and spacing evenly apart. Place a round label in the center of each ribbon that has been printed with the word "Ho!"...so festive!

Happy Family Casserole

Amy Swierkowski
Chappell Hill, TX

*This is one of the best recipes my mom made when I was young. It
has now become a favorite of my family of 6!*

4 c. biscuit baking mix
1 c. plus 4 T. milk
2 eggs, beaten
2 T. dried parsley
1 T. garlic powder
1 T. Italian seasoning

1 c. shredded Cheddar cheese
1/2 c. grated Parmesan cheese
8 slices American cheese
Garnish: grated Parmesan
     cheese, dried parsley

Combine biscuit baking mix, eggs, milk and seasonings; stir in
Cheddar and Parmesan cheeses and mix well. Spread half of the
mixture in a 13"x9" baking pan; top with Ground Beef Sauce and
American cheese. Spread remaining mixture on top; sprinkle with
additional Parmesan cheese and parsley. Bake at 325 degrees for
20 minutes. Makes 4 to 6 servings.

Ground Beef Sauce:

1 lb. ground beef, browned
1/2 c. onion, chopped
16-oz. can tomato sauce
4-oz. can mushrooms, drained
1 clove garlic, minced
1 t. sugar

1/2 t. dried oregano
1/2 t. dried basil
1/2 t. salt
1/2 t. pepper
1 bay leaf

Combine all ingredients in a saucepan and bring to a boil; reduce heat
and simmer for 15 minutes. Remove and discard bay leaf.

*Take a child to the grocery store to help choose dinner
ingredients with all the fixings to drop off at a local
food pantry…a tradition well worth keeping.*

☆ Season's Eatin's ☆

Spaghetti with Peas & Ham

Jody Bolen
Ashland, OH

*This pasta can be assembled quickly with ingredients
that are usually on hand.*

1/4 c. butter
1 T. all-purpose flour
1/4 t. salt
1/4 t. pepper
1-1/2 c. milk
1 c. shredded mozzarella cheese

10-oz. pkg. frozen peas, cooked
   and drained
1/4 lb. sliced deli ham, cut into
   1/8-inch strips
8-oz. pkg. spaghetti, prepared

Melt butter in a saucepan; stir in flour, salt and pepper. Add milk and
heat on low until slightly thickened. Stir in cheese and peas; heat and
stir until cheese is melted. Stir in ham and heat through. Toss with
warm spaghetti. Serves 6 to 8.

A simple box of photos taken throughout the years makes
the very best "coffee table" conversation starter.

Whole Baked Ham

Jacqueline Kurtz
Reading, PA

*A yummy ham that can be served hot or refrigerated
and sliced for sandwiches.*

12 to 14-lb. fully cooked boneless or semi-boneless ham
12 whole cloves
1-1/2 c. pineapple juice
1/2 c. maple-flavored syrup

6 slices canned pineapple
1 c. water
3/4 c. brown sugar, packed
3 T. mustard

Place ham, fat side up, in a shallow roasting pan. Press cloves into top of ham; stir together pineapple juice and syrup and pour over ham. Arrange pineapple slices on ham. Bake at 325 degrees for 1-1/2 hours. Add water and bake for 1-1/2 additional hours. Remove from oven; remove pineapple slices. Mix together brown sugar and mustard; spread over ham. Bake an additional 30 minutes. Makes 18 to 20 servings.

Play holiday music quietly during family dinners…try jazz, contemporary and country themes and find your family's favorites.

✳ Season's Eatin's ✩

Cheesy Sausage-Zucchini Casserole

Linda Behling
Cecil, PA

What fond memories I have of my mom, dad, sister, grandmas, and grandpas sitting around the kitchen table enjoying this scrumptious meal prepared by my mom.

1 lb. ground sausage
1/4 c. onion, chopped
1 c. tomato, diced
4 c. zucchini, cubed
2 4-oz. cans sliced mushrooms, drained

1-1/2 c. prepared rice
8-oz. pkg. pasteurized process cheese spread, cubed
1/8 t. dried oregano
salt and pepper to taste

Heat and stir sausage and onion in a large skillet over medium heat until evenly browned; drain. Stir in tomato and zucchini; heat until tender. Stir in remaining ingredients and spread in a 13"x9" baking pan. Bake uncovered for one hour at 350 degrees, until bubbly. Makes 8 servings.

For extra-special giftwrap, photocopy favorite vintage game boards, dominoes or playing cards.

Cranberry-Glazed Pork Chops

Edward Smulski
Lyons, IL

This recipe also works well with chicken or turkey cutlets. Excellent with white rice!

4 boneless, thin-cut pork chops
1 T. oil
16-oz. can whole cranberry
    sauce

3/4 c. French salad dressing
4 t. onion soup mix

Sauté pork chops on both sides in oil in a large skillet for 10 minutes or until juices run clear. Combine cranberry sauce, salad dressing and soup mix in a microwaveable bowl. Cover and microwave on high about 2 minutes, until heated through. Serve cranberry mixture over pork chops. Makes 4 servings.

Stick adhesive-backed gold stars onto plain pillar candles for quick holiday decorations.

✳ Season's Eatin's ✩

Savory Chicken & Potatoes

Shelley Turner
Boise, ID

As you walk into the house, knowing dinner is ready is almost as delicious a feeling as the taste of this slow-cooker favorite.

1 onion, thinly sliced
4 to 5 potatoes, peeled and
    cubed
4 to 6 boneless, skinless chicken
    breasts

10-3/4 oz. can golden
    mushroom soup
1/2 t. dried marjoram

Arrange onion slices in bottom of slow cooker; add potatoes, then chicken. Spread soup over top; sprinkle with marjoram. Cover and cook on low setting for 7 to 8 hours until chicken and potatoes are tender. Makes 4 to 6 servings.

A new twist for gift packages…add a homemade pompom in place of a paper bow. Simply wind yarn tightly around a 4-inch cardboard square several times. Holding carefully, slide yarn off cardboard and tie in the center with an 8-inch length of yarn. Clip the looped ends and shake out to fluff.

Herb-Roasted Holiday Turkey

Vickie

So easy...just pop the turkey in a roasting bag!

1 T. all-purpose flour	2 T. oil
2 stalks celery, chopped	1 T. dried sage
1 carrot, chopped	1 t. dried thyme
1 onion, sliced	1 t. dried rosemary
12 to 16-lb. turkey	1 t. seasoned salt

Shake flour in a turkey-size oven bag; arrange in roasting pan at least 2 inches deep. Add vegetables to bag; set aside. Remove neck and giblets from turkey and reserve for another use; rinse turkey, pat dry and brush with oil. Combine herbs and salt; sprinkle over turkey. Place turkey in bag on top of vegetables; close bag with nylon tie provided and tuck ends into pan. Cut six 1/2-inch slits in top of bag; insert meat thermometer into thickest part of inner thigh. Roast 2 to 2-1/2 hours at 350 degrees, until meat thermometer reads 180 degrees. Let stand in bag for 15 minutes before opening; pour off drippings and reserve for gravy. Serves 8 to 10.

Turkey Gravy:

drippings from roasted turkey	1/4 t. salt
1/4 c. all-purpose flour	1/4 t. poultry seasoning

Pour drippings into a large deep bowl. Spoon off fat, reserving 3 to 4 tablespoons; discard remaining fat. Measure drippings; add water if necessary to equal 2-1/2 cups. Place reserved fat in a skillet; stir in flour, salt and seasoning. Heat over medium-high heat, stirring constantly until smooth and bubbly, about one minute. Gradually stir drippings into flour mixture; heat to boiling, stirring frequently. Boil for 5 to 7 minutes until thickened. Makes about 2 cups.

✳ Season's Eatin's ✩

Angel Hair Chicken Pasta

Nancy Willis
Farmington Hills, MI

Such a tasty pasta dish!

1/4 c. butter
.7-oz. pkg. Italian salad dressing
  mix
1/2 c. white wine or chicken
  broth
10-3/4 oz. can golden
  mushroom soup

4-oz. pkg. chive & onion
  flavored cream cheese,
  softened
6 boneless, skinless chicken
  breasts
16-oz. pkg. angel hair pasta,
  prepared

Melt butter in a sauce pan; add dressing mix, wine or broth and
soup. Blend in cream cheese until smooth. Arrange chicken in a
13"x9" baking pan; pour mixture over chicken. Bake for 60 minutes at
325 degrees. Serve warm chicken and sauce over hot pasta. Serves 6.

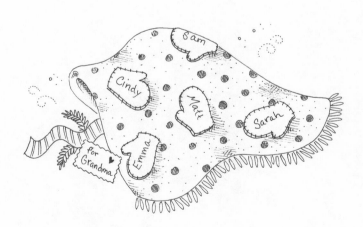

Stitch a cozy surprise for Grandma. Trim a store-bought
fleece throw with fleece mitten shapes that have been
embroidered with the grandkids' names…so thoughtful
(and easy!).

Easy Mexican Bake

Christi Sidney
Panama City, FL

Add a pound of browned ground beef to the beans for a heartier meal...toss a salad and dinner is ready!

16-oz. can refried beans
1/2 c. sour cream
3 c. tortilla chips, broken
10-oz. can diced tomatoes with
   chiles, drained

1 c. shredded Mexican blend
   cheese
Garnish: sour cream, lettuce,
   chopped tomatoes, chopped
   onions

Combine beans and sour cream in a saucepan over medium heat; heat through. Arrange chips evenly in an ungreased 13"x9" baking pan. Spread bean mixture lightly over chips; top with tomatoes and sprinkle with cheese. Bake uncovered at 350 degrees for 30 minutes, until cheese is bubbly. Garnish as desired. Serves 3 to 4.

Add a bit of elegance to your holiday open house...type up the menu and place in a gold frame. Place at the beginning of the buffet table with a bit of holly tucked into the frame.

✫ Season's Eatin's ✫

Mock Lasagna Casserole

Kathy Slevoski
North Hampton, NH

A tasty twist on an old favorite.

1 lb. ground sausage, browned
　and crumbled
15-oz. can tomato sauce
1/2 t. garlic salt
1/2 t. pepper

1/2 t. dried basil
1/2 c. water
7-oz. pkg. ziti pasta, prepared
1-1/2 c. cottage cheese
6 to 8 slices American cheese

Combine sausage, sauce, seasonings, and water in a medium saucepan; cover and simmer for 15 minutes, stirring occasionally. In a 2-quart baking dish layer half each of the pasta, cottage cheese, American cheese and meat sauce; repeat. Bake at 375 degrees for 30 minutes. Makes 4 servings.

Need a punch bowl in a pinch? Place a sturdy bowl upside-down on the table then set a larger bowl right-side-up on top. Yellowware bowls often come in a variety of designs and are eye-catching when stacked.

Mozzarella Chicken

Ruth Nein
Pennside, PA

My favorite family recipe...quick, easy and delicious.

6 boneless, skinless chicken
   breasts
6 slices mozzarella cheese
10-3/4 oz. can cream of chicken
   soup

1/4 c. water
1 c. herbed stuffing mix,
   crushed
1/8 c. margarine, melted

Arrange chicken in a 13"x9" baking pan; top each piece with a slice of cheese. Combine soup and water, mixing well; pour over cheese. Sprinkle stuffing mix crumbs over top and drizzle with margarine. Bake 55 to 60 minutes at 375 degrees. Makes 6 servings.

Dress-up doll ornaments! Gather little snippets of tulle, netting or satin and attach to paper dolls with costume jewelry earrings and pins...a sweet gift for any little girl on your list.

☆ Season's Eatin's ☆

Slow-Cooker Ham & Potatoes

Tina Coss
Winter, WI

A tasty, easy way to enjoy your holiday ham!

4 potatoes, peeled and sliced
2 onions, chopped
1-1/2 c. ham, cubed
2 T. butter
2 T. all-purpose flour

1/2 t. pepper
10-3/4 oz. can Cheddar cheese
  soup
1-1/3 c. water

Layer potatoes, onions and ham in a slow cooker; set aside. Melt butter in a saucepan; stir in flour and pepper until smooth. Combine soup and water; gradually add to flour mixture. Bring to a boil; heat and stir until thickened and bubbly. Pour over ham; cover and cook on low setting for 8 to 9 hours. Serves 4 to 6.

Stack straight-sided hurricanes with bright red and green shiny apples or fresh pears…it's a natural.

Polenta with Tomato

Gail Prather
Bethel, MN

Polenta is an Italian version of cornmeal mush…it's good, try it!

1/2 c. cornmeal
1/2 c. cold water
1-1/2 c. boiling water
1/2 t. salt
1 onion, chopped

1 clove garlic, chopped
2 T. fresh marjoram, divided
1 tomato, sliced
2 T. crumbled Gorgonzola
  cheese

Mix cornmeal with cold water in a 2-quart saucepan; stir in boiling water and salt. Cook, stirring constantly, until mixture thickens and boils. Reduce heat, cover and simmer for 10 minutes. Remove from heat; cool to room temperature. Stir in onion and garlic; spread in a greased 13"x9" baking pan. Sprinkle with one tablespoon marjoram. Cover; refrigerate for at least 6 hours. Cut into 6 squares and arrange on a greased baking sheet. Bake at 425 degrees for 5 minutes; top each square with one tomato slice. Sprinkle with remaining marjoram and cheese; bake for 5 to 7 minutes or until cheese begins to melt. Serve warm. Makes 6 servings.

Fresh scents for the holidays! Pierce small holes in limes using a toothpick, then fill each hole with a whole clove. Tie a ribbon all the way around, leaving a loop for hanging on a doorknob or the Christmas tree.

✴ Season's Eatin's ☆

Christmas Eve Pot Roast

Kristine Marumoto
Sandy, UT

*This is the best pot roast I have ever made! Easy, and fills the house
with the most wonderful, mouth-watering aroma.*

2 t. salt
1/2 t. pepper
1 t. paprika
1 t. garlic powder
4 to 5-lb. boneless chuck roast
3 T. all-purpose flour
2 T. oil
2/3 c. water

2 bay leaves
3 onions, quartered
5 carrots, peeled and quartered
4 potatoes, peeled and quartered
14-1/2 oz. can Italian-style
    diced tomatoes with juice
15-oz. can tomato sauce

Blend seasonings in a small bowl; rub into roast and coat with flour.
Heat oil in a heavy saucepan or Dutch oven; add roast and brown
briefly on all sides over high heat. Add water and bay leaves to pan;
cover, reduce heat to low and simmer for 2 hours. Add remaining
ingredients, cover and simmer for an additional hour. Remove and
discard bay leaves. Makes 6 to 8 servings.

Christmas...that magic blanket that wraps itself about us.

-Augusta E. Rundell

Chicken & Chipped Beef

Terri Simmons
Blue Springs, MO

*Years ago, I worked with a lady from Atlanta who shared these
wonderful recipes that taste fantastic, look pretty
and are, best of all, super easy to make.*

4-1/2 oz. jar dried, chipped beef,
   cut into small pieces
8 boneless, skinless chicken
   breasts
8 slices bacon, partially cooked

10-3/4 oz. can cream of
   mushroom soup
10-3/4 oz. can cream of chicken
   soup
2 16-oz. containers sour cream

Sprinkle chipped beef in bottom of a 13"x9" baking pan. Wrap a bacon
slice around each chicken breast; arrange in pan. Mix soups and sour
cream; spread over chicken and bake at 250 degrees for 3-1/2 hours.
Serve with Christmas Rice. Makes 8 servings.

Christmas Rice:

1 bunch green onions, chopped
4-oz. can sliced mushrooms,
   drained
1/2 c. butter
3 c. prepared rice

4-oz. jar chopped pimentos,
   drained and patted dry
8-oz. can sliced water chestnuts,
   drained and chopped

In a medium saucepan, sauté onions and mushrooms in butter. Add
remaining ingredients, mix well and heat through over low heat.

make a joyful noise!

☆ Season's Eatin's ☆

Pizza Pasta

Jennifer Clingan
Dayton, OH

All your favorite pizza flavors in a casserole! Easy to change to suit your family's tastes...substitute turkey sausage, eliminate the pepperoni, add other vegetables as you like. Yum!

1-lb. pkg. ground Italian
   sausage
1 c. onion, chopped
8-oz. pkg. spiral pasta, prepared
8-oz. mushrooms, sliced
4-oz. pkg. sliced pepperoni

15-oz. jar pizza sauce
1/2 green pepper, chopped
2-1/4 oz. can sliced black olives,
   drained
8-oz. pkg. shredded mozzarella
   cheese

Brown sausage and onion in a skillet; drain and transfer to a 13"x9" baking pan. Set aside. Combine pasta, mushrooms, pepperoni, pizza sauce, pepper and olives; spoon over sausage. Sprinkle with cheese; cover and bake at 350 degrees for 45 minutes. Uncover and bake for an additional 5 to 10 minutes. Serves 8.

For a warm glow at dinner, place a floating candle in
a water-filled wine glass at each place setting.

Turnaround Turkey & Rice

Theresia King
Knoxville, TN

A wonderful way to use leftover holiday turkey! Served with steamed broccoli and hot buttered rolls, it's sure to become a family favorite.

2 T. butter
2 stalks celery, chopped
1 onion, chopped
1 c. turkey, cooked and cubed
1-1/2 c. water

1/4 c. milk
.87-oz. pkg. turkey gravy mix
2 T. all-purpose flour
1 t. seasoned salt
2 c. prepared long-cooking rice

Melt butter in a saucepan over medium heat. Add celery and onion; heat and stir for 5 minutes or until tender. Stir in turkey. Blend together water, milk, gravy mix, flour and salt in a bowl; stir into turkey mixture. Bring to a boil; reduce heat and simmer for 5 minutes, until thickened and warmed through. Serve over rice. Makes 2 to 4 servings.

Paint an old-fashioned wooden barrel in red & white stripes, line with a big plastic bag and add a balled real tree this year...plant outside after the holidays to enjoy the tree year 'round.

✦ Season's Eatin's ✦

Mom's One-Pot Pork Chop Dinner

Kim Allen
New Albany, IN

A nice break from all the turkey, ham and prime rib!

1 T. butter	1 onion, sliced
4 pork chops	10-3/4 oz. can cream of
3 potatoes, peeled and sliced	mushroom soup
2 c. baby carrots	1/4 c. water

Melt butter in a skillet over medium heat and brown pork chops for
3 to 5 minutes on each side. Add potatoes, carrots and onion to skillet.
Combine soup and water; pour over meat and vegetables, cover and
simmer for 15 to 20 minutes or until vegetables are tender. Makes
4 servings.

Let it snow, let it snow, let it glow! Pack the snow lining the
front walkway into mounds around bright red or green
votives and light the way to a warm welcome.

Dad's Pork & Cabbage

Karen Puchnick
Butler, PA

Happy New Year's Day...start the year off right
with a meal of pork & cabbage for luck!

1 T. oil
1 lb. boneless pork, cut into thin
   strips
1 T. butter
1/2 head cabbage, shredded
1 onion, diced
2 t. caraway seed

1 red pepper, cut in strips
1 green pepper, cut in strips
1/2 c. white wine or chicken
   broth
1 c. chicken broth
salt and pepper to taste

Heat oil in a large skillet; add pork and sauté until browned. Remove pork to a bowl. Add butter to the skillet; reduce heat to medium, add cabbage and sauté until wilted. Add onion and continue heating until onion is tender. Stir in caraway seed, salt, pepper and wine or 1/2 cup broth; raise heat and simmer until most of the liquid has evaporated. Pour in one cup chicken broth; return to a boil, then reduce to a simmer. Return pork to the skillet; add peppers, cover and simmer until the peppers are crisp-tender. Stir well and serve with prepared noodles or spaetzle. Serves 3 to 4.

Create a clever corkboard for showing off your holiday cards. Paint the wooden frame of a bulletin board in Christmas red acrylic paint and use vintage Scrabble® pieces to spell out "Happy Holidays!" along the border.

Home Sweet Home

Yummy Desserts

Coconut-Almond Fudge Bars

Roberta Schuler
Gooseberry Patch

*Place bars in holiday-decorated mini muffin cup liners for
an oh-so-simple holiday sweet.*

2 c. fudge cake mix
16-oz. tub coconut-almond
    frosting

1 c. applesauce
1 egg

Mix all ingredients together; pour into a greased and floured
13"x9" baking pan. Bake at 350 degrees for 30 to 32 minutes; cut
into 2-inch squares. Makes 3 dozen.

Easy Chocolate-Coconut Cake

Eileen Cole
Bloomingburg, NY

*Cans of cream of coconut are usually near the grenadine syrup and
other cocktail mixes at the grocery store!*

18 1/2-oz. chocolate cake mix
15-oz. can cream of coconut
16-oz. pkg. frozen whipped
    topping, thawed

Optional: chocolate shavings

Bake cake in a tube pan according to package directions; remove from
pan while still warm. Poke holes in cake with the handle of a wooden
spoon; pour cream of coconut into holes and let cool completely.
Spread with whipped topping and sprinkle generously with chocolate
shavings, if desired. Serves 10 to 12.

✫ Home Sweet Home ✫

Busy Moms' Peach Cobbler

Terri Miles
Grayville, IL

Top with vanilla ice cream for a frosty treat that's so easy to make!

18 1/2-oz. yellow cake mix
   with pudding
1/2 c. butter, melted

29-oz. can peaches with juice
cinnamon to taste

Empty cake mix into a mixing bowl. Pour butter over mix and stir until texture is crumbly; set aside. Place peaches with juice in a greased 13"x9" baking pan; sprinkle with cake mixture, then with cinnamon. Bake at 350 degrees for 30 to 35 minutes, until golden and bubbly. Makes 10 to 12 servings.

A delicious treat anyone will enjoy! Melt a bag of semi-sweet chocolate chips, and dip pretzels, raisins, crackers, marshmallows, peanut brittle, pecans, dried fruit or espresso beans. Pack into holiday tins for giving.

Gingerbread Cookie Mix in a Jar

Kelly Alderson
Erie, PA

Don't forget to tie on a gingerbread boy cookie cutter, too!

3-1/2 c. all-purpose flour,
   divided
1 t. baking powder
1 t. baking soda
2 t. ground ginger

1 t. ground cloves
1 t. cinnamon
1 t. allspice
1 c. brown sugar, packed

Mix 2 cups flour, baking powder and baking soda in a bowl. In a second bowl mix the remaining flour and the spices. Layer as follows in a one-quart, wide-mouth canning jar, packing firmly between layers: flour-baking powder mixture, then brown sugar, and finally the flour-spice mixture. Attach the following instructions.

Instructions:

Empty contents of jar into a large mixing bowl; stir to blend. Use hands to mix in 1/2 cup softened butter, 3/4 cup molasses and one slightly beaten egg. Cover and chill for one hour. Roll chilled dough to 1/4-inch thickness on a lightly floured surface and cut into shapes with cookie cutters. Arrange cookies 2 inches apart on lightly greased baking sheets. Bake for 10 to 12 minutes at 350 degrees. Cool on wire racks; decorate as desired. Makes about 1-1/2 dozen.

Whoever heard of a regular home without a cookie jar?
'Twould be a drab situation indeed!

- Alice Child

☆ Home Sweet Home ☆

Congo Bars

Dee Rogers
South Charleston, WV

A guaranteed kid-approved treat!

1 c. margarine, melted
2-1/4 c. brown sugar, packed
3 eggs

2-1/2 c. self-rising flour
12-oz. pkg. semi-sweet
   chocolate chips

Mix margarine and brown sugar together; add eggs one at a time, beating well after each. Slowly stir in flour and chocolate chips; spread into a greased 13"x9" baking pan. Bake at 350 degrees for 35 minutes; cool completely before cutting into bars. Makes 2 dozen.

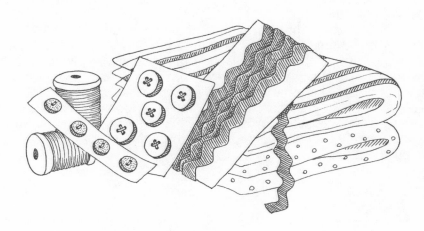

House guests coming for the holidays? Spruce up spare blankets by edging with an easy blanket stitch or a border of rick-rack tacked into place.

Candied Fruitcake

Marie Needham
Columbus, OH

My friend, Gerry, shared this recipe with me in the early 1960's. These fruitcakes are nearly all fruit and nuts with just enough batter to hold them together.

3 7-1/2 oz. pkgs. pitted dates, chopped
16-oz. pkg. candied pineapple, chopped
16-oz. pkg. whole candied cherries
2 c. all-purpose flour
2 t. baking powder
1/2 t. salt
4 eggs, beaten
1 c. sugar
2 16-oz. pkgs. pecan halves

Combine dates, pineapple and cherries in a large bowl. Stir together flour, baking powder and salt in a second bowl; pour onto fruit mixture. Mix well with hands; separate pieces so that all are well coated. In another bowl, blend eggs with a hand mixer until frothy; gradually blend in sugar. Add to fruit mixture; mix well with a large spoon. Add pecans; mix with hands until evenly distributed and coated with batter. Grease two 9" springform pans or two 9"x5" loaf pans; line with parchment paper cut to fit, then grease paper. Spread mixture in pans; press mixture down with hands; rearrange pieces of fruit and nuts as necessary to fill up any empty spaces. Bake for 1-1/4 to 1-1/2 hours at 275 degrees; tops will look dry when done. Remove from oven; cool for 5 minutes on wire racks; turn out onto racks, carefully peel off paper and cool thoroughly. Store loosely wrapped. Makes 2 cakes.

☆ Home Sweet Home ☆

Monster Cookies

Janie Branstetter
Fairview, OK

My daughter's favorite cookie! This recipe makes a huge amount...perfect for holiday cookie exchanges and parties.

4 c. sugar
2 16-oz. pkgs. brown sugar
16-oz. pkg. margarine
12 eggs
3 16-oz. jars peanut butter
4 t. vanilla extract
2 T. plus 2 t. baking soda

18 c. quick-cooking oats, uncooked
16-oz. pkg. semi-sweet chocolate chips
16-oz. pkg. candy-coated chocolates
16-oz. pkg. chopped nuts

Cream together the sugars, margarine, eggs and peanut butter in a very large bowl; stir in baking soda and vanilla. Add remaining ingredients and mix well. Spoon onto greased baking sheets and bake at 350 degrees for 10 to 15 minutes. Makes 18 dozen cookies.

Turn cut-outs into ice cream sandwiches...spread softened ice cream on one cookie and top with another cookie. Roll edges of ice cream in coarsely chopped red & white peppermint candies and freeze until solid.

Whatever Bars

Rhonda Phillips
Sand Springs, OK

My favorite aunt gave me this recipe. You can make it whatever flavor you like just by using a different flavor of cake mix, hence the name.

18-1/2 oz. lemon cake mix
3/4 c. butter
1-1/4 c. chopped pecans,
   divided

8-oz. pkg. cream cheese,
   softened
1 c. brown sugar, packed

Mix together cake mix, butter and one cup pecans; spread in a greased 13"x9" baking pan. Blend cream cheese and brown sugar and spread over mixture; sprinkle with remaining pecans. Bake at 350 degrees until light golden, 25 to 30 minutes. Makes 2 to 3 dozen.

Sprinkle snowflake-shaped glitter onto a clear glass plate, then top with another glass plate to hold glitter in place...so sweet to serve cookies from!

✩ Home Sweet Home ✩

Scottish Shortbread

Laurie Copeland
Williamson, NY

Make these sparkle by sprinkling with coarse, colored sugar while still warm.

1/2 c. butter
6 T. sugar

1-1/2 c. all-purpose flour
1/8 t. salt

Cream butter and sugar; gradually add flour and salt. Press into an 11" round cake pan; prick the edges with a fork. Bake at 325 degrees for 17 to 20 minutes until golden. Cut into wedges. Makes one dozen.

Viennese Crescents

Gail Collins
Woodstock, MD

My best friend of almost 30 years and I get together each Christmas to bake cookies. These have been our favorites for years!

1-2/3 c. all-purpose flour
1/3 c. sugar
1 c. finely ground pecans
1/4 t. salt

1 c. butter, softened
1 t. vanilla extract
Garnish: powdered sugar

Mix flour, sugar, nuts and salt using hands; work in butter and vanilla until mixture holds together. Chill for one hour. Shape into crescents; place on ungreased baking sheets and bake for 10 to 12 minutes at 350 degrees. Cool and roll in powdered sugar. Makes 3 to 4 dozen.

Fast Chocolate Fondue

Michelle Campen
Peoria, IL

Your guests will love dipping cake cubes, macaroons, pretzels,
bananas and strawberries in this sweet fondue!

2 T. butter
1 c. semi-sweet chocolate chips
14-oz. can sweetened
   condensed milk

1 t. vanilla extract
Garnish: assorted dippers

Melt butter and chocolate in a heavy saucepan over low heat, stirring occasionally. Stir in milk and extract; heat, stirring constantly, about 5 minutes or until smooth and hot. Serve warm in a fondue pot, small saucepan or heat-resistant bowl set over low heat or hot water; surround with dippers. Makes 8 servings.

Surprise a crafty friend with a jazzy journal! Dress up the cover of a blank journal with scrapbooking paper, buttons, charms and bits of ribbon…"sew" cute!

Home Sweet Home ✧

Apple Gingerbread Squares

Jo Ann

Love the taste of gingerbread but not the mess of cookies? Then this dessert is for you!

1/4 c. butter
1/3 c. brown sugar, packed
1/3 c. molasses
1/2 c. orange juice
1 egg
1-1/4 c. all-purpose flour
1 t. baking soda

1 t. cinnamon
1 t. ground ginger
1/4 t. ground cloves
1/4 t. salt
1 Golden Delicious apple, peeled, cored and chopped
Optional: powdered sugar

Melt butter in a medium saucepan over medium heat. Add brown sugar, molasses and orange juice; whisk until blended. Remove from heat; stir in egg. Combine flour, baking soda, spices and salt; stir into molasses mixture just until combined. Stir in apple. Pour into a greased, floured 8"x8" baking pan; bake at 350 degrees for 25 to 30 minutes or until center is firm. Cut into squares; sprinkle with powdered sugar, if desired. Serve warm. Makes 8 servings.

Dip pretzel rods in melted chocolate, then coat with chopped nuts and crushed peppermint candies…arrange in a holiday glass filled with coarse sugar for a stand-up treat.

Zesty Lemon Squares

Cheryl Walker
North Syracuse, NY

Sweet, refreshing and did I say sweet?!

1 c. butter, softened	2 c. sugar
2-1/4 c. all-purpose flour	1/3 c. lemon juice
1/2 c. powdered sugar	1/2 t. baking powder
4 eggs, beaten	Garnish: powdered sugar

Cut butter into flour and sugar until mixture kneads together; press
into an ungreased 13"x9" baking pan. Bake at 350 degrees for
20 minutes or until golden; remove from oven. Mix together
remaining ingredients and pour over baked crust. Bake at 350 degrees
for an additional 20 to 25 minutes. Sprinkle with powdered sugar and
cut into bars. Makes 2 to 3 dozen.

A truffle tree…poke a toothpick halfway into a foil-wrapped
truffle and the remaining half into a styrofoam tree form.
Continue until form is filled…a chocolate-lover's dream.

Home Sweet Home

Blythe's Ho-Ho Cake

Blythe Friedley
Marblehead, OH

Easier than it looks and incredibly delicious!

1-3/4 c. all-purpose flour
2 c. sugar
3/4 c. baking cocoa
1-1/2 t. baking soda
1-1/2 t. baking powder
1 t. salt

2 eggs
1 c. milk
1/2 c. oil
2 t. vanilla extract
1 c. boiling water

Stir together first 6 ingredients. Add next 4 ingredients; blend with hand mixer 2 minutes on medium. Stir in water. Grease and flour sides of two 13"x9" baking pans; line bottoms with wax paper. Divide batter between pans. Bake for 15 to 20 minutes at 350 degrees; test for doneness. Cool completely. Place one cake on a tray; spread with Creamy Filling and top with second cake. Pour Chocolate Frosting over top (or spread with canned frosting); chill. Serves 12 to 15.

Creamy Filling:

3/4 c. milk
2-1/2 T. all-purpose flour
3/4 c. butter

1 c. sugar
1 t. vanilla extract

Combine milk and flour in a saucepan. Cook on medium heat, stirring until thickened; set aside. Blend butter for 4 minutes with a hand mixer; add sugar and blend 4 minutes. Stir in milk mixture and vanilla; blend an additional 4 minutes.

Chocolate Frosting:

1/2 c. butter, melted and cooled
1 egg
1 t. vanilla extract

2 T. baking cocoa
2-1/2 T. hot water
2 c. powdered sugar

Blend all ingredients together; will be thin. Chill to set, if necessary.

Chocolate Cherry Bars

Helene Gibson
Las Vegas, NV

My mother has made these bars at the holidays for many years...so quick & easy and they are gobbled up fast.

18-1/2 oz. pkg. devil's food
    cake mix
2 eggs

1 t. almond extract
14-1/2 oz. can cherry pie filling

Combine cake mix, eggs and almond extract and mix well. Stir in pie filling until moist. Pour into greased 13"x9" baking pan and bake at 350 degrees for 20 to 25 minutes or until done. Remove from oven and cool completely. Spread with Chocolate Frosting and cut into squares. Makes 2 dozen.

Chocolate Frosting:

1-1/2 c. powdered sugar
6 T. butter, softened
6 T. milk

1/2 c. semi-sweet chocolate
    chips

Combine sugar, butter and milk in a saucepan; heat to boiling and boil for one minute. Remove from heat; add chocolate chips, stir until smooth and use immediately.

Forgot the centerpiece? Cut some twigs and branches and bring indoors. Arrange in a sturdy container and place gumdrops, cranberries and mini marshmallows on the ends of the branches for a unique gumdrop tree.

✦ Home Sweet Home ✦

Farmhouse Cut-Out Cookies

Beverly Fortner
North Manchester, IN

Set out frostings, jimmies and sugars...let everyone decorate!

1 c. shortening
2 c. sugar
2 eggs
1 c. sour cream
1 t. vanilla extract

4-1/2 c. all-purpose flour
4 t. baking powder
1/2 t. baking soda
1/2 t. salt
Garnish: frosting

Blend shortening, sugar, eggs, sour cream and vanilla together well; set aside. Combine dry ingredients in a second bowl; stir into shortening mixture. Chill dough for an hour. Roll out 1/2-inch thick on floured surface and cut out with desired cookie cutters. Arrange on lightly greased baking sheets. Bake at 350 degrees for 12 minutes. Cool for 2 to 3 minutes on baking sheets; remove to wire racks to finish cooling. Frost as desired. Makes 4 to 5 dozen.

Get a head start on your holiday open house. Bundle up silverware in cloth napkins a few days in advance and then just place in a big basket...all ready to go to the table when you are!

Finnish Nisu

Dee Dee Warden
Delaware, OH

This traditional Finnish sweet bread is delightful served warm, with butter. For a shortcut, make according to bread machine instructions.

1 pkg. active dry yeast
1/2 c. warm water
2 c. milk, scalded and cooled to
   lukewarm
1 c. sugar
1 t. salt
7 to 8 whole cardamom pods,
   seeded and crushed

5 eggs, beaten, divided
8 to 9 c. all-purpose flour,
   divided
1/2 c. butter, melted
Optional: 1/2 c. chopped
      almonds, 1/2 c. coarse sugar

In a large mixing bowl dissolve yeast in warm water; stir in milk, sugar, salt, cardamom, 4 eggs and enough flour to make a batter, about 2 cups. Beat until dough is smooth and elastic. Add 3 additional cups of flour and blend well; dough should be quite smooth and glossy. Add melted butter and stir well; beat again until dough looks glossy. Add the remaining flour until a stiff dough forms.

Turn out onto a lightly floured board and cover with an inverted mixing bowl; let rest 15 minutes. Knead until smooth and satiny. Place in a lightly greased mixing bowl; turn dough to grease the top, cover lightly and let rise in a warm place until double in bulk, about one hour. Punch down and let rise again until almost double, about 30 minutes.

Turn out again onto a lightly floured board; divide into 3 parts, then divide each into 3. Shape each into a strip about 16 inches long by rolling dough between palm of hand and board. Braid 3 strips together into a straight loaf, pinch ends together, and tuck under. Repeat to make 2 more loaves. Place the loaves on lightly greased baking sheets; let rise for about 20 minutes, until puffy but not double in size. Brush with remaining beaten egg; sprinkle with almonds and coarse sugar. Bake at 400 degrees 25 to 30 minutes or until light golden; do not overbake. Slice to serve. Makes 3 loaves.

Home Sweet Home

Cranberry-Almond Crunch Cookies

Carol Hickman
Kingsport, TN

Dip half of each cookie in melted white chocolate and set aside until firm....an extra holiday touch.

1 c. butter, softened
1 c. sugar
1 c. brown sugar, packed
1 egg, beaten
1 c. oil
1 t. vanilla extract

3-1/2 c. all-purpose flour
1 t. baking soda
1/2 t. salt
2 c. cranberry-almond cereal, crushed
1 c. white chocolate chips

Cream butter and sugars together; add egg, oil and vanilla. Set aside. Combine flour, baking soda and salt; stir into creamed mixture. Mix in cereal and chocolate chips; shape dough into one-inch balls. Place on ungreased baking sheets; flatten with a fork. Bake at 325 degrees for 15 minutes; cool on baking sheets one minute. Cool completely on wire racks. Makes about 10 dozen.

Dress up your holiday cookies...drizzle with melted white or semi-sweet chocolate and sprinkle with chopped, dried cherries. Extra special and extra tasty!

Forgotten Cookies

Bethany Zemaitis
Pittsburgh, PA

*An old-time favorite from my great-grandmother. Once the cookies
are in the oven, you really can just forget them until later!*

2 egg whites
2/3 c. sugar
1 c. chopped walnuts

12-oz. pkg. semi-sweet
chocolate chips

Preheat oven to 350 degrees. Beat egg whites until stiff; gradually add
sugar and beat until mixture forms peaks. Fold in nuts and chocolate
chips. Drop by teaspoonfuls onto baking sheets and place in oven.
Turn oven off and leave cookies in oven until oven is cold; do not
peek. Makes 3 dozen.

For a kids-only party, use a colorful fleece scarf as the table
runner. Tuck forks & spoons into matching mittens to give
as take-home gifts.

Home Sweet Home

Chunky Chocolate Cookie Mix in a Jar

*Laura Fuller
Fort Wayne, IN*

A simple gift to give to teachers, caregivers and others.

1-3/4 c. all-purpose flour	1/2 c. sugar
1 t. baking soda	1/4 c. baking cocoa
1 t. baking powder	1/2 c. chopped walnuts
1/4 t. salt	1 c. semi-sweet chocolate
3/4 c. brown sugar, packed	chunks

Mix together the flour, baking soda, baking powder and salt; set aside.
Layer brown sugar, sugar and cocoa in a one-quart, wide-mouth jar,
packing down firmly between layers. Add nuts and chocolate chunks;
pack down firmly and top with flour mixture. Attach the following
instructions.

Instructions:

Pour contents of jar into a large mixing bowl; blend thoroughly. Add
3/4 cup softened butter, one slightly beaten egg and one teaspoon
vanilla extract. Mix until completely blended; use hands to finish
mixing. Shape into walnut-size balls and place 2 inches apart on
parchment paper-covered baking sheets. Bake at 350 degrees for
11 to 13 minutes; cool 5 minutes on baking sheets, then place on wire
racks to finish cooling. Makes 3 dozen.

Have a super kid? Here's a super gift!
Decoupage a plain-colored desk
lampshade with comic-book images.
Sure to please, no matter what the age.

Peppermint Candy Cheesecake

Bobbi Carney
Centennial, CO

*Drizzle strawberry syrup on each slice right before serving
for a merry little touch.*

1 c. graham cracker crumbs
3/4 c. sugar, divided
6 T. butter, melted and divided
1-1/2 c. sour cream
2 eggs
1 T. all-purpose flour
2 t. vanilla extract

2 8-oz. pkgs. cream cheese,
   softened
1/4 c. candy canes, coarsely
   crushed
Garnish: frozen whipped
   topping, thawed; crushed
   candy canes

Blend crumbs, 1/4 cup sugar and 1/4 cup melted butter in bottom of
ungreased 8" round springform pan; press evenly over bottom. Blend
sour cream, remaining sugar, eggs, flour and vanilla in a blender or
food processor until smooth. Add cream cheese and blend; stir in
remaining 2 tablespoons melted butter until completely smooth.
Fold in crushed candy and pour over crust. Bake at 325 degrees for
45 minutes. Remove from oven; cool, then refrigerate for 4 hours or
overnight. Loosen pan sides and remove springform; serve garnished
with whipped topping and crushed candy. Makes 12 servings.

Turn peat pots from the nursery into silver mantel
cups... simply spray paint with shiny silver acrylic paint,
embellish with holiday wishes in dimensional paint, and
tuck in small bunches of herbs.

☆ Home Sweet Home ☆

Anise Loaf

Betty Wilson
Columbus, OH

If pizzelles are a favorite, you're sure to like this original dessert.

1/2 c. margarine, softened
2 to 3 c. sugar, to taste
4 eggs, beaten
4 c. all-purpose flour
4 t. baking powder

1/2 t. salt
2/3 c. water
2 T. anise oil
1 c. oil

Blend together margarine, sugar and eggs; set aside. Combine flour, baking powder and salt in a separate bowl; add dry ingredients and water alternately to margarine mixture and blend well. Stir in oils. Pour into 2 greased and floured 9"x5" loaf pans. Bake at 325 degrees for approximately one hour; test centers for doneness. Store wrapped in plastic wrap, then in aluminum foil. Makes 2 loaves.

A homemade checkerboard that will bring smiles, win or lose…decoupage a grandchild's picture over every other square of a prepainted checkerboard. Copy and reduce pictures, if necessary, using a color photocopier.

Chocolate Crunch Brownies

Lisa Willard
Dunwoody, GA

*Chocolate, peanut butter, marshmallow creme...all the essentials
of a sweet-tasting treat!*

1 c. butter, softened
2 c. sugar
4 eggs
6 T. baking cocoa
1 c. all-purpose flour
2 t. vanilla extract

1/2 t. salt
7-oz. jar marshmallow creme
1 c. creamy peanut butter
2 c. semi-sweet chocolate chips
3 c. crispy rice cereal

Cream together butter and sugar in large mixing bowl; add eggs,
then stir in cocoa, flour, vanilla and salt. Spread into a greased
13"x9" baking pan; bake at 350 degrees for 35 to 40 minutes, until
a toothpick comes out clean. Cool; spread with marshmallow creme
and set aside. Mix peanut butter and chocolate chips in a saucepan
over low heat, stirring constantly. Remove from heat; stir in cereal.
Spread on top of marshmallow layer and refrigerate; cut into bars.
Makes 2 to 3 dozen.

Easy placecards...bend a 12" green pipe cleaner into a
triangular tree shape, twisting the ends together at the
center of the base to form the trunk. Insert the trunk into
a cork and pin on a namecard with a bulletin board tack.
So simple and fun for kids to do!

Home Sweet Home

Triple Chocolate Delight

Theresa Oliver
Ovalo, TX

Top with vanilla ice cream or whipped topping...or both!

18-1/2 oz. pkg. chocolate
  cake mix
3.9-oz. pkg. instant chocolate
  pudding mix
2 c. sour cream

1 c. water
1/2 c. oil
4 eggs, beaten
6-oz. pkg. semi-sweet chocolate
  chips

Mix all ingredients well and pour into a greased slow cooker. Cook for 6 to 8 hours at low setting. Makes 8 to 10 servings.

Satin Slipper Pie

Pat Habiger
Spearville, KS

What a cute name...and a yummy pie!

20 marshmallows
1/2 c. milk
6 1.55-oz. milk chocolate candy
  bars

1 c. whipping cream
9-inch pie crust, baked
Garnish: toasted almonds

Combine marshmallows, milk and chocolate in a saucepan; heat until melted. Set aside to cool. Whip cream until stiff peaks form; fold into mixture. Pour into pie crust; chill until firm. Garnish with toasted almonds. Serves 6 to 8.

Sweet & Simple Bread Pudding

Athena Colegrove
Big Springs, TX

Chunks of apple or banana make a sweet addition to this
slow-cooker recipe. Top with warm cream.

3 c. bread cubes
1/2 c. raisins
3/4 c. brown sugar, packed
3 eggs, beaten

3-1/2 c. milk
2 t. vanilla extract
2 t. cinnamon
1/2 t. salt

Mix all ingredients together until bread cubes are thoroughly soaked.
Place in a lightly greased slow cooker; cook on high setting for
3 to 4 hours until a knife inserted into the middle comes out clean.
Serve warm or cold. Makes 6 to 8 servings.

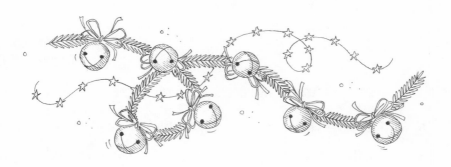

Mix & match dishes, serving platters, silverware and table
linens during the holidays…each place setting will add
its own sparkle just as each guest will.

✫ Home Sweet Home ✫

Frosty Snowballs

Jessica Parker
Mulvane, KS

*The secret ingredient is the big glass of icy milk to serve
right along with these cookies.*

1 c. butter, softened
1/3 c. sugar
1 T. water
1 t. vanilla extract

2-1/4 c. all-purpose flour
1 c. chopped pecans
1 c. powdered sugar, divided
sugar sprinkles in 3 colors

Blend butter with a hand mixer for 30 seconds; add sugar. Stir in
water and vanilla until well combined; mix in flour and pecans. Shape
dough into one-inch balls; place on ungreased baking sheets. Bake at
325 degrees for 20 minutes; cool. Place 1/3 cup of powdered sugar
into each of 3 bowls; add sprinkles to each bowl. Gently roll and shake
cookies in powdered sugar mixture. Makes 3 dozen.

Decorate evergreen boughs with mini lights and
place in galvanized buckets…a cheery
front porch welcome.

Chocolate Quesadillas

Joshua Logan
Corpus Christi, TX

Sprinkle with cinnamon & sugar too...mmmmm good!

6 8-inch flour tortillas
2 T. butter, melted

1 c. milk chocolate chips
Garnish: vanilla ice cream

Brush both sides of each tortilla with melted butter; arrange in a single layer on an ungreased baking sheet. Sprinkle chocolate chips on half of each tortilla; fold over tortillas. Bake for 4 to 6 minutes at 450 degrees until golden. Top each with a scoop of vanilla ice cream. Makes 6.

Too sweet...wrap packages in plain red wrapping paper and glue a row or 2 of wrapped red & white peppermints all across the top.

✩ Home Sweet Home ✩

Snickerdoodles Mix in a Jar

Megan Brooks
Antioch, TN

An old favorite...kids love it just for the funny name!

2-3/4 c. all-purpose flour	2 t. cream of tartar
1/4 t. salt	2 c. sugar, divided
1 t. baking soda	1 T. cinnamon

Combine flour, salt, baking soda, cream of tartar and 1-1/2 cups sugar in a large bowl; mix well and pack in a one-quart, wide-mouth canning jar. Combine remaining sugar and cinnamon in a small plastic zipping bag; attach to jar along with the following instructions.

Instructions:

Cream together one cup butter and 2 eggs in a large mixing bowl. Pour in the cookie mix and stir until a dough forms. Shape dough in walnut-size balls; roll in sugar-cinnamon mixture in bag and arrange 2 inches apart on ungreased baking sheets. Bake for 10 to 15 minutes at 350 degrees until cookies are golden. Cool on wire racks. Makes 3 dozen.

A narrow velvet ribbon tied around a linen napkin, with a sprig of holly peeking out, reflects a feeling of simple hospitality.

Walnut Crunch Pumpkin Pie

Judy Voster
Neenah, WI

This brings back special memories of evenings spent shelling nuts with my mother. What a good time we would have...the jokes and laughter flew faster than the nutshells!

16-oz. can pumpkin
12-oz. can evaporated milk
2 eggs
3/4 c. brown sugar, packed
1-1/2 t. cinnamon
1/2 t. salt

1/2 t. ground ginger
1/2 t. nutmeg
9-inch pie crust
Garnish: frozen whipped
    topping, thawed

Blend pumpkin, milk, eggs, brown sugar, spices and salt in a large bowl with hand mixer at medium speed until well mixed. Place pie plate with crust on oven rack; pour in pumpkin mixture. Bake at 400 degrees 40 minutes or until a knife inserted one inch from the edge comes out clean. Cool; sprinkle topping evenly over pie. Change oven to broiler setting. Place pie 5 to 7 inches below broiler and broil about 3 minutes or until topping is golden and sugar dissolved. Cool on wire rack; garnish with whipped topping. Makes 10 servings.

Walnut Topping:

1 c. chopped walnuts
3/4 c. brown sugar, packed

4 T. butter, melted

Mix ingredients well in a small bowl.

Candy cane lane...glue candy canes, curved side out, around the outside of a clean coffee can for a quick flower vase.

Visions of Sugarplums

HOME-MADE candy

A handy candy temperature chart:

230 to 233 degrees = thread stage

234 to 243 degrees = soft ball stage

244 to 249 degrees = firm ball stage

250 to 269 degrees = hard ball stage

270 to 289 degrees = soft crack stage

290 to 310 degrees = hard crack stage

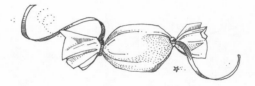

Chocolate Truffles

Vickie

Wrap up in colorful foil papers for a festive assortment.

3/4 c. butter
3/4 c. baking cocoa
14-oz. can sweetened
   condensed milk
1 T. vanilla extract

Garnish: baking cocoa,
   powdered sugar, chopped
   nuts, candy sprinkles, flaked
   coconut

Melt butter in heavy saucepan over low heat; add cocoa and stir until smooth. Add sweetened condensed milk; cook and stir constantly until mixture is thick, smooth and glossy, about 4 minutes. Remove from heat; stir in vanilla. Cover and refrigerate 3 to 4 hours or until firm. Shape into 1-1/4 inch balls; roll in desired garnish. Refrigerate again until firm, one to 2 hours. Store, covered, in refrigerator. Makes 2-1/2 dozen.

Visions of Sugarplums

Bourbon Balls

Jennifer Halsmer
Franklin, IN

Roll in baking cocoa or fine, colored sugars as well.

2 T. baking cocoa
1 c. powdered sugar
2 c. vanilla wafers, crushed
1 c. chopped pecans

1/4 c. bourbon or 2 to 4 t.
   vanilla extract
2 T. light corn syrup
Garnish: powdered sugar

Sift together cocoa and powdered sugar; stir well. Add wafer crumbs and pecans; mix well. Stir in bourbon or vanilla and corn syrup; mix well. Shape into balls and roll in powdered sugar; allow to dry before serving. Makes 3 dozen.

So easy, so clever…nestle Bourbon Balls in
mini muffin liners, putting one in each section
of a vintage ornament box.

Mom's Microwave Fudge

Julie Perkins
Anderson, IN

For peanut butter fudge, simply substitute 1/2 cup peanut butter for the baking cocoa.

1-lb. pkg. powdered sugar
1/2 c. butter
1/4 c. milk

1/2 c. baking cocoa
1 T. vanilla extract

Combine all ingredients in a microwave-safe bowl. Microwave on high setting for 3 minutes; remove, stir well and blend in nuts. Spread in a greased 8"x8" pan. Chill; cut into squares. Makes about 5 dozen.

White Christmas Fudge

Sue Wadsworth
Lufkin, TX

Gently press holiday-shaped jimmies onto the top before firm...how merry!

3 c. sugar
1/2 t. cream of tartar
1/4 t. salt
1 c. light cream
1 T. butter

1-1/2 t. vanilla extract
1/2 c. chopped nuts
1/4 c. chopped dates
1/4 c. chopped red and green
   candied cherries

Combine sugar, cream of tartar, salt and cream in a heavy saucepan. Bring to a boil; brush down sides of pan with a moistened pastry brush. Boil, without stirring, until mixture reaches the soft-ball stage, or 234 to 243 degrees on a candy thermometer. Remove from heat, add butter and cool, without stirring, to 110 degrees on a candy thermometer. Add vanilla, nuts and fruit; beat until mixture starts to thicken. Spread in a greased 9"x9" baking pan. Chill; cut into squares. Makes about 6 dozen.

Visions of Sugarplums

Pounds of Fudge

Peggy Wulf
Franktown, CO

My mother, Jackie Camp, and I make 75 to 80 pounds of fudge every year!

1-1/2 c. margarine
6 c. sugar
1-1/2 c. evaporated milk
2 12-oz. pkgs. semi-sweet
   chocolate chips

13-oz. jar marshmallow creme
2 c. chopped pecans
2 t. vanilla extract

Mix margarine, sugar and evaporated milk in a heavy 4 to 5-quart saucepan. Bring to a full rolling boil on medium heat, stirring constantly. Continue to boil on medium heat for about 5 minutes until mixture reaches the soft-ball stage, 234 to 243 degrees on a candy thermometer. Remove from heat and stir in chocolate chips until melted; add marshmallow creme, nuts and vanilla and mix well. Spread in 2 lightly greased 13"x9" baking pans and cool at room temperature. Cut into squares. Makes 6 pounds.

Short on time? Scoop out one-inch balls of filling from a prepared cheesecake, place into mini muffin liners and insert round lollipop sticks. Drizzle with melted chocolate and caramel for a gourmet delight that's sure to impress.

Good-Old-Days Vinegar Taffy

Amy Moffatt
Trenton, MI

The secret to taffy is to lift edges with a fork and fold back into the center of the taffy to discourage any hardening before it's cool enough to handle.

2 c. sugar	1/8 t. cream of tartar
2 T. butter	1/8 t. salt
1/2 c. vinegar	

Combine all ingredients in a large saucepan; boil to hard-ball stage, or 250 to 269 degrees on a candy thermometer. Pour onto a buttered surface; cool just until comfortable to the touch. Find a partner and pull with buttered hands until taffy is white and porous. Cut with buttered scissors into one-inch pieces; wrap in wax paper. Makes about 2-1/2 dozen.

Glass-blown tree toppers make unique centerpieces when ends are placed in glass candlesticks…group them together for a rainbow of colors.

Visions of Sugarplums

Puffy Marshmallow Cut-Outs

Anna Burns
Delaware, OH

Perfect for s'mores when cut into graham cracker square size!

3/4 c. water	1/4 t. salt
4 envs. unflavored gelatin	2 t. vanilla extract
3 c. sugar	1-1/2 c. powdered sugar,
1-1/4 c. light corn syrup	divided

Spray a 13"x9" baking pan with non-stick vegetable spray. Line with wax paper; coat wax paper with non-stick vegetable spray and set aside. Pour water into a bowl and sprinkle gelatin over top; let stand 5 minutes. Place sugar, corn syrup, salt and vanilla in a heavy sauce-pan and bring to a boil. Cook over high heat until mixture reaches the soft-ball stage, 234 to 243 degrees on a candy thermometer. Beat the hot mixture slowly into the gelatin mixture for about 10 minutes or until very stiff. Pour into prepared pan; smooth top with a spatula. Set aside, uncovered, overnight until mixture becomes firm. Invert the baking pan on a surface coated with one cup powdered sugar; peel off wax paper. Lightly coat the insides of desired cookie cutters with non-stick vegetable spray and cut out marshmallows. Roll in remaining powdered sugar to coat. Makes about 2 dozen.

Gumdrops by the yard! String colorful construction paper circles and gumdrops for a quick & easy garland.

Cinnamon Almonds

Diana Chaney
Olathe, KS

Make by the bagfuls, they'll disappear fast.

1 egg white
1 t. cold water
4 c. whole almonds

1/2 c. sugar
1/4 t. salt
1/2 t. cinnamon

Lightly beat egg white; add water and beat until frothy but not stiff. Add almonds; stir until well coated. Mix sugar, salt and cinnamon in a small bowl. Sprinkle over almonds, toss to coat and spread evenly on a lightly greased baking sheet. Bake for one hour at 250 degrees, stirring occasionally, until golden. Cool; store in an airtight container. Makes 4 cups.

Cluster taper candles together with a ribbon, snuggle down into a wide glass vase filled with a few inches of Epsom salt...sparkly and welcoming.

Visions of Sugarplums

Candied Pecans

Marjorie Jergesen
Knoxville, TN

These should be called Magical Pecans…they disappear right before your very eyes!

1 t. cold water
1 egg white
1 lb. pecan halves

1 c. sugar
1 t. cinnamon
1/2 t. salt

Beat together water and egg white until frothy; add pecans and mix well. Combine sugar, cinnamon and salt; mix well with pecans. Spread on a greased baking sheet. Bake at 225 degrees for one hour, stirring occasionally. Makes one pound.

Glazed Cashews

Kerry Mayer
Dunham Springs, LA

Betcha can't eat just one!

2 c. whole cashews
1/2 c. sugar

2 t. butter
1/2 t. vanilla extract

Combine cashews, sugar, and butter in a saucepan over medium heat; stir until sugar turns a rich golden color. Remove from heat; stir in vanilla. Spread on a greased baking sheet to cool. Makes 2 cups.

Microwave Peanut Brittle

Amanda Jackson
Springfield, MO

So easy, so quick and mess free.

1-1/2 c. raw peanuts
1/2 c. corn syrup
1 c. sugar

1/8 t. salt
1 t. butter
1 t. vanilla extract
1 t. baking soda

Combine peanuts, corn syrup, sugar and salt in a microwave-safe 4-cup glass measuring cup. Microwave uncovered on high setting for 6 to 8 minutes, stirring halfway through cooking time; stir well at end of cooking time. Add butter and vanilla; mix well and heat an additional 1-1/2 minutes. Stir in baking soda. Pour onto greased baking sheet, cool and break into pieces. Makes about one pound.

Pecan Crunch

Jen Sell
Farmington, MN

This is just as tasty when made with almonds.

1/2 c. butter
1/2 c. sugar

1 c. coarsely chopped pecans
1 T. light corn syrup

Combine all ingredients in a skillet; bring to a boil and cook 5 minutes or until light brown. Spread on a buttered, aluminum foil-lined baking sheet. Cool for 15 minutes; break into pieces. Makes about one pound.

Visions of Sugarplums

Grandma's Peanut Brittle

Sue Schwoerer
Bloomington, IL

I continue my dear grandma's tradition of making peanut brittle for Christmas, and pack it in tins to send to my brothers and sister who live all over the country.

2 c. sugar
1 c. light corn syrup
1/2 c. water
1 lb. raw peanuts

1/8 t. salt
1 t. baking soda
1 t. vanilla extract
1 T. butter

Combine sugar, corn syrup and water in a large heavy aluminum or stainless steel saucepan; stir over medium heat until sugar dissolves and mixture is hot. Cover and heat an additional 3 minutes, until sugar crystals on sides of saucepan dissolve. If not dissolved after 3 minutes, brush the sides with a water-dipped pastry brush. Cook uncovered over medium heat to soft-ball stage, or 234 to 243 degrees on a candy thermometer, stirring often. Add peanuts and stir constantly; cook to hard-crack stage, or 290 to 300 degrees on a candy thermometer; watch thermometer carefully and do not exceed 300 degrees. Remove from heat; quickly stir in salt, baking soda, vanilla and butter. Pour out onto a greased baking sheet; spread as much as possible. Use greased forks or hands to carefully lift and pull edges of hot candy. Cut into pieces with greased kitchen scissors; lay on greased wire rack to cool. Continue around edges of baking sheet, lifting and pulling brittle as thin as possible. Cool and store in an airtight container. Makes about one pound.

Fill disposable frosting cones with layers of old-fashioned candies and tie closed with curling ribbon...sweets for the sweet!

Strawberry Popcorn

Lisa Hains
Tipp City, OH

*Once you try this, you'll just have to experiment with lime, lemon
and grape gelatin, too!*

4 pkgs. microwave popcorn,
   popped
1 c. water
2 c. sugar
3 T. butter

1 t. vanilla extract
2 t. strawberry gelatin mix
1/8 t. salt
several drops red food coloring

Place popcorn in a very large roasting pan or bowl; set aside. Mix
together remaining ingredients in a medium saucepan; boil for
10 minutes, stirring frequently. Pour mixture over popcorn; stir to mix.
Bake for one hour at 300 degrees, stirring several times; cool. Makes
about 2 gallons.

Caramel Corn

Angie O'Keefe
Soddy Daisy, TN

Of course, add peanuts, pecans or cashews if you'd like!

8 c. popped popcorn
3/4 c. brown sugar, packed
6 T. butter

3 T. light corn syrup
1/4 t. salt

Place popcorn in a very large roasting pan or bowl; set aside. Combine
remaining ingredients in a heavy saucepan. Heat and stir until
mixture starts to boil. Continue cooking for 5 minutes, stirring often.
Remove from heat and pour over popcorn; toss to coat. Bake at
300 degrees for 15 minutes; stir, return to oven and bake an additional
5 to 10 minutes. Turn out onto aluminum foil; cool and break into
small pieces. Makes 2 quarts.

⋆ Visions of Sugarplums ⋆

Popcorn Balls

Kimberly Lutrick
Abernathy, TX

I wrap these in colorful plastic wrap, tie with festive ribbon and place
them in a little sleigh by our fireplace...a festive decoration
AND a festive snack!

5 qts. popped popcorn
2 c. sugar
1-1/2 c. water
1/2 c. light corn syrup

1 t. vinegar
1/2 t. salt
1 t. vanilla extract

Place popcorn in a large roasting pan; keep warm at 250 degrees in
oven. Combine sugar, water, corn syrup, vinegar and salt in a heavy
saucepan. Heat over medium heat, stirring until sugar is dissolved and
mixture reaches hard-ball stage, or 250 to 269 degrees on a candy
thermometer. Remove from heat; add vanilla and stir well. Pour over
warm popcorn; butter hands and form into balls. Wrap in plastic wrap.
Makes 15 to 20.

Caramels

Melissa Maneval
West Unity, OH

Chewy, buttery goodness!

1 c. butter
2 c. brown sugar, packed
1/8 t. salt
1 c. light corn syrup

14-oz. can sweetened
  condensed milk
1 t. vanilla extract

Melt butter in a 3-quart saucepan. Add sugar and salt; stir thoroughly.
Stir in corn syrup and mix well. Gradually add condensed milk; stir
constantly over medium heat until mixture reaches the firm-ball stage,
or 244 to 249 degrees on a candy thermometer. Remove from heat;
stir in vanilla. Pour into a well-greased 9"x9" pan. Cool; cut into small
squares and wrap in wax paper. Makes about 6 dozen.

Hard Tack Candy

Joyce Keirns
Bradenton, FL

*Once you make one batch, there will be requests
for all kinds of flavors!*

3-3/4 c. sugar
1-1/2 c. light corn syrup
1 c. water

several drops flavored oil for
candy making
several drops food coloring

Mix together sugar, corn syrup and water in a saucepan; stir over medium heat until sugar dissolves. Heat to boiling and cook until it reaches the hard-crack stage, or 290 to 310 degrees on a candy thermometer. Remove from heat; stir in flavoring and coloring. Pour over a baking sheet dusted with powdered sugar; cool. Cut into pieces while still slightly warm. Makes 2 pounds.

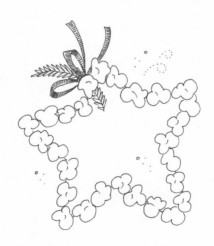

Star light, star bright. Place a well greased star-shaped
open cookie cutter on a greased aluminum foil-lined
baking sheet. Fill with coarsely chopped peppermint candies
and bake at 325 degrees until candy melts. Gently push out
of form…pretty swirled candy stars!

Visions of Sugarplums

Red Rock Candy

Yvonne Higgins
Franklin, NH

A cinnamon favorite…add red food coloring for an even more vibrant red!

2 c. sugar
1 c. light corn syrup
1/2 c. water

1/2 c. red cinnamon candies
1 t. butter

Combine sugar, corn syrup and water in a saucepan; cook over low heat, stirring until sugar dissolves. Cook to soft-ball stage, or 234 to 243 degrees on a candy thermometer. Stir in cinnamon candies; cook to hard-ball stage, or 250 to 269 degrees on a candy thermometer, stirring frequently. Remove from heat and add butter; stir slightly. Pour onto a greased baking sheet. When cool, break into pieces. Makes about a pound.

A peppermint tree…hot glue individually wrapped
red & white candies tightly together on a styrofoam cone.
The wrapper ends will be pushed outward
and glisten in the light.

Golden Mix

Vicki Adams
New Bethlehem, PA

*Deliver a tin of Golden Mix along with a movie to a special
friend...take time to enjoy all three, the movie, the mix
and the company.*

4-1/2 c. bite-size crispy rice or
    corn cereal squares
4 c. popped popcorn
1/2 c. whole cashews
1/4 c. butter

6 T. brown sugar, packed
2 T. light corn syrup
1/4 c. vanilla extract

Mix cereal, popcorn and nuts in a large roasting pan; set aside. Heat
remaining ingredients to boiling in a 2-quart saucepan over medium
heat, stirring frequently. Pour over cereal mixture, stirring until evenly
coated. Bake at 250 degrees for 45 minutes; stir every 15 minutes.
Spread on wax paper to cool; stir occasionally to break up. Store in
airtight container. Makes 9-1/2 cups.

Trim a tea party tree...tie dainty teacups to the ends of
branches, gather lacy hankies and clip onto tree using
vintage costume jewelry pins. Dangling teaspoons and
tea caddies add even more charm and sparkle.

Visions of Sugarplums

Crunching Snow Snack Mix

Kathy Grashoff
Fort Wayne, IN

A tasty treat to enjoy on the drive to Grandma's house!

9 c. mixed bite-sized crispy
   cereal squares
1 c. salted mini pretzel twists
1 c. peanuts

1 c. marshmallows
1 c. raisins
1 c. dried fruit
2 lbs. white melting chocolate

Mix together all ingredients except chocolate and set aside. Melt chocolate in a microwave or double boiler; stir thoroughly until melted. Pour chocolate over dry ingredients; mix together with a large spoon. Spread in a thin layer on wax paper. When cool, break into small pieces. Store in airtight container. Makes about 16 cups.

Smitten with mittens? String together a pair of woolen mittens with a narrow ribbon and hang from a peg alongside a Santa hat…how jolly!

Maple Cream Candy

Cyndi Little
Whitsett, NC

Creamy goodness wrapped up in chocolate.

1/2 c. butter
2 T. maple flavoring
16-oz. pkg. powdered sugar
2 to 3 t. water

12-oz. pkg. semi-sweet
  chocolate chips
1/3 bar paraffin wax
Optional: pecan halves

Cream together butter and flavoring until mixed well; add sugar and mix well. Add water one teaspoon at a time, mixing well until mixture resembles play clay. Pinch off pieces and roll into one-inch balls; flatten and place on a wax paper-lined baking sheet. Refrigerate for at least 30 minutes. Melt chocolate chips and paraffin in a double boiler; stir until blended. Use a toothpick or candy dipper to dip maple candy balls into chocolate, coating completely. Top with pecan halves, if desired. Chill until chocolate is set. Store in an airtight container. Makes 5 to 6 dozen.

Secret Ingredient Candy

Lillian Kane
Dansville, NY

Try it, no one will ever guess the secret ingredient!

3 T. mashed potatoes
3 c. powdered sugar

1-1/2 c. creamy peanut butter

Stir mashed potatoes into powdered sugar; mix well and add a little more potato as needed to make a dough the consistency of pie crust. Roll out into an 1/8-inch thick rectangle on a board coated with powdered sugar. Spread evenly with peanut butter. Roll tightly along the longer side of the rectangle, jelly-roll style. Wrap in plastic wrap; refrigerate at least 2 hours. Slice 1/2 inch thick. Store in an airtight container. Makes about 2 dozen.

Visions of Sugarplums

Never-Fail Divinity

Karrie Middaugh
Salt Lake City, UT

*Stir dried, chopped cherries, pineapples or apricots into the
marshmallow creme before adding the hot mixture
to satisfy that sweet tooth!*

1/2 c. water
2 c. sugar
1/8 t. salt

7-oz. jar marshmallow creme
1/4 c. chopped nuts

Combine water, sugar and salt in saucepan; bring to rolling boil and
cook for 2 minutes. Place marshmallow creme in large mixing bowl;
pour hot mixture over marshmallow creme. Stir until mixture loses its
gloss; add nuts and mix well. Drop by teaspoonfuls onto wax paper.
Makes 1-1/2 pounds.

Fill a footed bowl with colorful, shiny bulb ornaments and
lots of jingle bells...oh-so fun and easy.

Cherry Speckles

Liza Linaweaver
Plains, KS

*These chocolate-speckled candies are equally good
when raspberry gelatin mix is used.*

3 egg whites
1/8 t. salt
3-1/2 T. cherry gelatin mix
3/4 c. sugar

1 t. vinegar
1 c. semi-sweet chocolate chips

Use an electric mixer to beat egg whites and salt in a glass mixing bowl until foamy; set aside. Mix gelatin and sugar together; gradually add to egg white mixture and beat until peaks form. Stir in vinegar; fold in chocolate chips. Drop by teaspoonfuls close together on aluminum foil-lined baking sheet. Bake at 250 degrees for 25 minutes; turn oven off and leave in oven 20 additional minutes. Makes about one pound.

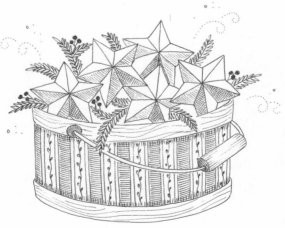

Everyone appreciates an extra-special journal. Glue an old-fashioned postcard to the front of a plain spiral-bound notebook and then tuck a candy cane through the spiral.

Visions of Sugarplums

Cranberry Snack Mix

Jodie Blevins
Vandenberg AFB, CA

A crunchy treat that's fun to share. Try substituting walnuts or pecans for variety.

1 c. whole almonds
2 c. mini pretzel twists
1 c. sweetened, dried cranberries
1 egg white

1/2 c. sugar
1/2 t. cinnamon
1/2 t. salt

Combine nuts, pretzels and cranberries; set aside. Beat egg white in a small bowl until foamy; pour over nut mixture. Mix remaining ingredients in another small bowl; sprinkle on nut mixture and toss until well coated. Spread evenly on a greased baking sheet. Bake for one hour at 225 degrees, stirring every 15 minutes. Cool completely on baking sheet. Store in airtight container. Makes 4 cups.

Wrap up individual candies in a variety of colors of cellophane and then add to a glass canister...a jar full of tasty jewels!

English Toffee

Rochelle Sundholm
Creswell, OR

Sprinkle with coarsely chopped red & white peppermints or toffee chips for an extra-special delight.

1 c. butter
1-1/3 c. sugar
1 T. light corn syrup
3 T. water

2-1/2 c. toasted blanched
   almond bits, divided
2 to 3 1.55-oz. milk chocolate
   candy bars

Combine butter, sugar, corn syrup and water in a large heavy saucepan. Heat, stirring occasionally, until mixture reaches the hard-crack stage or 300 degrees on a candy thermometer. Remove from heat and stir in 1-1/2 cups almond bits; spread in a well-greased 13"x9" baking pan; cool. Melt chocolate bars; turn cooled candy out onto wax paper and spread with half the chocolate. Sprinkle with one-half cup of the remaining almond bits; let candy set. Turn over and spread other side with remaining chocolate; sprinkle with remaining almond bits. Chill until firm; break into pieces. Makes about 3 pounds.

Pecan Turtles

Lisa Lindsey
Limestone, ME

There's nothing slow about these turtles...they disappear quickly!

14-oz. pkg. caramels, wrappers
   removed
1/4 c. evaporated milk
2 c. pecan halves

1/4 bar paraffin wax
6-oz. pkg. semi-sweet chocolate
   chips

Melt caramels and evaporated milk together in medium saucepan over low heat; add nuts. Drop by teaspoonfuls onto buttered wax paper; refrigerate until firm. Melt chocolate chips and paraffin together in medium saucepan over low heat; dip candies into chocolate and return to wax paper. Makes about 2 pounds.

Deck the Halls

Easy-to-make decorations

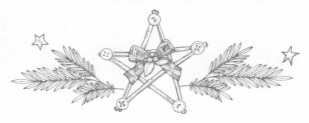

Garlands Galore

Hang over doorways, tie on on chair backs from spindle to spindle, wrap around the tree or tuck behind mirror and picture frames...garlands are the hugs of holiday decorating!

Woolly Welcome

jingle bells
desired length heavy thread
darning needle

2"x2" felted wool squares in
  holiday colors, figure about
  60 sqs. per foot

Tie 3 jingle bells to one end of thread; string on about 60 felted squares, one on top of the other. Add a cluster of 2 or 3 bells; add another section of felted squares. Continue until desired length is achieved; tie off with a cluster of jingle bells.

Gossamer Ribbon Chain

6-inch lengths gossamer ribbon   clothespins
craft glue

Curl one length ribbon into a circle; secure closed with a dot of glue and hold with clothespin until glue dries. Loop the next ribbon through the first, link-style and secure with a dot of glue. Continue until desired length is achieved.

Vintage Tie-able

assortment of reproduction or
  vintage die-cut holiday cards

desired length evergreen-colored
  one-inch wide satin ribbon

Punch one hole on each of the 2 horizontal sides of the cards; string ribbon down through one hole, across the back and up through the remaining hole. Slide card to desired distance; attach remaining cards, knotting ribbon on the back sides if necessary to hold cards in place.

☆ Deck the Halls ☆

Colonial Tinfoil Trim

desired length heavy-duty
    aluminum foil, 12 inches
    wide

scissors

Fold length of aluminum foil in half horizontally; cut three-quarters
of the way through every one inch along the folded side toward the
unfolded side. Turn around; cut in the center of each previous cut
three-quarters of the way from the unfolded edge toward the folded
edge. Gently unfold and pull each end to open. Hang immediately.

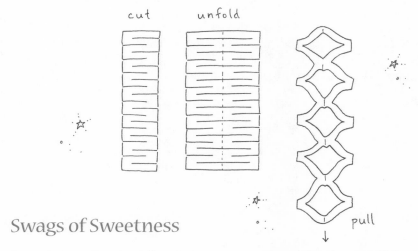

Swags of Sweetness

assortment of cellophane-
    wrapped candies, mini
    wrapped candy canes, sour
    balls

stapler with staples

Lay out candies, end to end, in a fun pattern for about a 4-foot length.
Simply staple together, end to end, through the cellophane wrappers.
Gently hang, keeping wrapped candy away from any lighted bulbs
on the tree.

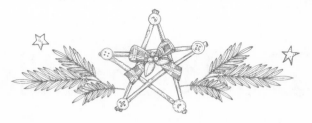

All Aglow

The flicker of candlelight warms the coldest of evenings and calms the flurry that seems to go hand-in-hand with the holidays.

Bright Placecards

4 clear glass coffee mugs
4 glass votive jars, about
    1/2-inch in diameter smaller
    than mug interior
1 c. coffee beans

4 hazelnut or vanilla-scented
    votive candles
4 mini candy canes
4 8-inch lengths ribbon
4 hang tags

Place one votive jar in the center of each mug; add coffee beans to fill space between votive jar and mug. Tuck a candy cane into coffee beans; arrange a candle in each votive. Tie a bow onto each handle. Write names on each hang tag and tie into bow. Set at each place setting. Makes 4.

Bowls of Wonder

heat-resistant glass serving
    bowl
several cups sand, Epsom salt or
    sugar to fill selected bowl
    2/3 full

5 tapered candles
sequins

Place serving bowl at desired location; fill 2/3 full with sand, Epsom salt or sugar. Insert tapers at slight angles, pushing until secure. Sprinkle sequins over sand, Epsom salt or sugar until covered.

✲ Deck the Halls ✲

Custom Candles

desired holiday pictures from
postcards, stickers or holiday
wrapping paper
sheets of clear matte computer
labels
scissors

plain-colored pillar candle
small garden urn or terra cotta
pot large enough to fit
diameter of candle
sprigs of fresh rosemary, thyme
or evergreen

Transfer image to clear matte labels using a color copier; trim the
pictures with scissors and adhere to the side of the candle. Place
candle in an urn or terra cotta pan; tuck herb sprigs or greenery
around the bottom.

Candletop Parfaits

cranberries
kumquats
4 parfait glasses

4 votive candles
4 to 8 sprigs fresh rosemary

Layer cranberries, kumquats and then cranberries again in each parfait
glass. Nestle a votive into the center of the top layer of cranberries.
Add a few sprigs rosemary around bottom of votive. Place at each
setting, or arrange in a row right down the middle of the
dessert table.

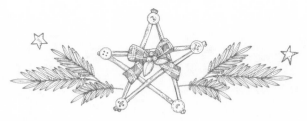

Tree-mendous Holidays

One for the table, one for the hall, but one for each, that's best of all!

All-About-Me Tree

cone-shaped styrofoam topiary
   form
6-inch dowel rod, 1/4 inch in
   diameter
terra cotta pot
florist's foam
hot glue gun and glue

assortment of tiny personalized
   trinkets like puzzle pieces,
   plastic jewelry, crayons,
   badges, small toys, buttons,
   ribbons and hair bows
paper or cardboard star

Insert one end of dowel into base of tree and opposite end into florist's foam. Place in the terra cotta pot. Use hot glue to glue trinkets all over tree form, covering well. Add more trinkets to cover florist's foam. Write name of recipient on star; glue to tree top.

Deck the Halls

Gift Tree

assortment of boxes in
    graduated sizes
assorted plain and patterned
    green wrapping papers

assorted ribbons and bows
tree skirt
ornaments
star-shaped or angel ornament

Wrap each box in different green wrapping paper; add ribbons. Stack in desired location in a tree shape, from largest on the bottom to smallest on the top. Decorate with bows and an assortment of ornaments perched on the ledges created by stacking the boxes. Top with star or angel ornament.

Boa-utiful Tree

15"x5" styrofoam cone
2 2-yd. white feather boas
florist's pins

craft glue
6-inch white feather dove

Beginning at bottom of cone, wrap and secure first feather boa with pins coated in glue about every 4 inches. Continue in a spiral fashion, securing second feather boa in the same way. Pin or glue dove to top of tree.

Countdown Fun

Count down the days to Christmas with a new delight everyday! Have fun making these countdown crafts and then enjoy sharing the surprises with your little ones!

First Christmas

24 baby socks or 12 pairs
   brightly colored children's
   holiday socks

4-ft. length ribbon
24 mini clothespins
24 small surprises

Lay out socks in a row all facing the same direction, spacing about 2 inches apart; stretch out ribbon above socks. Adjust spacing and clip socks to ribbon with mini clothespins. Hang up along a mantel; tuck a surprise into each. Starting on December 1st, take one down each day and let your child remove the surprise. Clip the sock back up facing the other direction…everyone can easily see the holiday approaching.

Photo Hang-Ups

2 3-ft. lengths medium-gauge
   wire
4 suction cup hangers
24 favorite photos of year round
   occasions

craft glue
numbers 1 through 24 cut out
   from lightweight cardboard
24 metal clips with rings

Wind ends of wire around suction cup stems; stick to any clean, smooth surface, stretching until taut. Arrange pictures in desired order; glue a number from one to 24 onto the back of each photo. Use clips to mount pictures backwards along wires, keeping in order from one to 24. Flip over one picture each day to count down happy faces and places until Christmas.

☆ Deck the Halls ☆

Simple Messages

24 envelope-size sheets of paper
green and red fine-point
   markers
12 small red envelopes
12 small green envelopes

length of jute to fit mantel
24 mini clothespins
50 4"x1" strips assorted
   homespun

Write a message, poem, quote or activity on each slip of paper; place one in each envelope. (Some examples to get you started: "Name Santa's reindeer," "Let's make cookies today!") Stretch and attach jute across mantel or desired location. Number envelopes from one to 24, alternating green and red; seal. Hang envelopes along jute using mini clothespins; knot 2 strips of homespun before each envelope and on both ends of jute. Encourage your child to open one envelope each day before Christmas and read the special message.

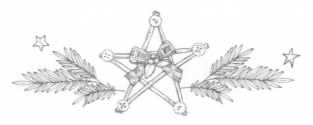

Natural Wonders

Look all around...you can find the most marvelous materials for crafting in the nature that surrounds us everyday.

Star Bright

paper
pencil
twigs

sharp knife or pruning shears
chenille stems

Draw a 5-pointed star of desired size on a piece of paper; lay twigs over the star shape. Trim twigs to correct size, if necessary. Wrap pieces of chenille stems around twigs at points to hold star together.

Wheat Bundle

3-inch thick bundle of wheat
florist's wire

ribbon

Cut three-fourths of the wheat to the desired length plus one inch, since it will be slightly shorter when twisted. Trim remaining wheat one inch shorter. Gather longer wheat by handfuls, keeping heads straight and stems untwisted. Tap lightly on a table so ends remain even; continue until all longer wheat is bundled. Wrap two-thirds of the way up with florist's wire; surround with shorter wheat and secure with wire. Twist bundle to form an hourglass shape; tighten wire. Tie ribbon to hide wire; stand bundle upright.

☆ Deck the Halls ☆

Woodland Topiary

2 cans spray paint
6-inch pail or terra cotta pot
hot-glue gun and glue
8-inch styrofoam ball

6"x6" sq. styrofoam
mixed large nuts
smaller nuts, seeds and berries

Spray paint pail or terra cotta pot desired color; set aside until dry. Glue styrofoam ball onto styrofoam square; place inside pail or pot, trimming edges if necessary. Remove from pail. Beginning at the bottom edge of the ball, hot glue large nuts to surface; continue until ball is covered as completely as possible. Hot glue smaller nuts and seeds in between large nuts until surface is covered. Spray paint the whole topiary silver or gold, if desired. Place back into pail or pot, hot gluing in place for added stability.

Feathered Friend Feeders

4" to 8" wooden star
yellow acrylic paint
drill
48-inch length jute
large crafting needle

grapefruit, halved
birdseed
apple, halved
peanut butter

Paint star; set aside to dry. Drill hole in a point of the star large enough for jute to fit through; string jute through hole, knotting to secure. Scoop center of fruit from grapefruit halves; string through the bottom center of the grapefruit halves onto the jute. Slide to desired spacing, knotting underneath to keep in place. Add apple halves in same manner. Tie a loop on the end of the jute and hang from a tree branch. Smear apple halves with peanut butter and sprinkle with birdseed; fill grapefruit halves with birdseed.

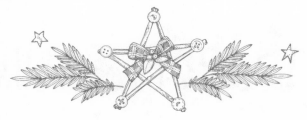

Frozen Delights

The sparkle of ice twinkles like diamonds...turn the yard into a glistening welcome!

Rings of Ice & Holly

Bundt® or other round tube pan
water
holly leaves

red berries
sprigs of greenery
jute

Fill pan half full with water; place in the freezer or outdoors until frozen solid. Arrange holly, berries and greenery on top; fill pan to top with water. Freeze solid; dip pan in hot water and invert to remove ice form. Hang up from a tree branch by looping jute through the center of the form and up and over a tree branch.

✫ Deck the Halls ✫

Fire & Ice

star-shaped soap molds	greenery
desired size crock for outdoors	votive candles
crushed ice	

Fill molds with water; freeze. Store in freezer until desired amount are made. Fill a crock with crushed ice or snow; insert greenery. Tuck ice stars into greenery and nestle votive candles in front. Set outdoors and light candles for a warm welcome.

I will honor Christmas in my heart and try to keep it
all the year.

-Charles Dickens

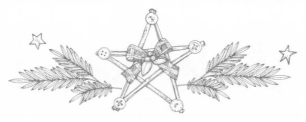

Simply Stockings

Hung by the chimney with care...and filled with goodies.

Enlarge template on page 209 to desired size on a copier; add a
1/2-inch seam allowance all around. Place fabric right-sides together;
cut out 2 stocking shapes. Matching right sides, leaving the top edge
open and using a 1/2-inch seam allowance, pin and sew together
along the stocking edges. Clip curves and turn right side out, using
a spoon to help push out and shape curves. Add a ribbon loop; fill
with gifts, trinkets and messages.

Cook's Stocking: use 2 tea towels as the fabric for this stocking.
Fill with a bundle of wooden spoons, spatula, recipe cards and packets
of spices.

Quilter's Stocking: use muslin as the stocking background; sew on a
variety of velvets, embroidering edges in a crazy-quilt pattern. Fill with
new scissors, fat quilt quarters, quilting pins, soft measuring tapes and
a thimble.

Bride-to-Be Stocking: use tulle for the stocking, adding a narrow
satin loop for hanging. Fill with soaps, sachets and mini toiletries.

Countdown Stocking: use felted wool with primitive stitching to
make small stockings for the tree; label from one to 24. Add a button
or 2 and a small rick-rack hanging loop, slip a tiny treat inside and
count down to Christmas.

✳ Deck the Halls ✳

Me-Oh-My, So Many Baubles, So Little Time

*Easier yet…buy a plain ready-made stocking and add a
little something to personalize it:*

* tassels of all kinds
* buttons, from little pearl ones to large pewter ones
* sparkling seed beads
* fringe
* pom-poms
* jingle bells
* rick-rack
* lace
* trinkets
* flea-market costume jewelry
* sequins

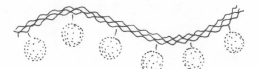

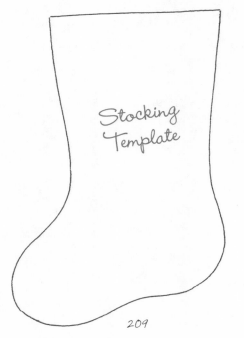

Stocking
Template

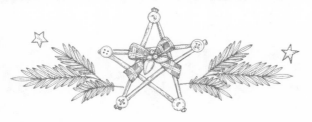

Holiday Hang-Ups

Dress up clear ornaments for trees, wreaths and more!

Keepsake Ornaments

round clear glass or acrylic
   ornaments with removable
   tops
heartfelt photos

photo computer paper
decorative-edged scissors
Optional: rubber cement

Scan a favorite family photo, changing the printer to copy in black & white. Reduce image to interior bulb size, about 3"x2"; print image. Cut out with decorative-edged scissors, leaving a white border around the edges. Remove ornament top; roll up image tightly and slide into ornament. Photo should uncurl. Secure photo in place with a dot of rubber cement if necessary; replace ornament top.

Razzled & Dazzled

tiny seed beads in desired color
   combinations
2" dia. florist's foam ball
craft glue

1" wide foam paintbrush
4-inch length ribbon
straight pin

Pour beads into a disposable bowl; set aside. Coat foam ball with glue using the foam paintbrush; roll in beads until coated. Set aside to dry; shake gently to remove any loose beads. Form ribbon into a loop; secure into the top of the ball with a straight pin dipped into glue.

✳ Deck the Halls ✳

Feather Light

round clear glass or acrylic
    ornaments with removable
    tops
white and silver glitter
fluffy white or pastel feathers

thin paintbrush
craft glue
white, pastel and clear seed
    beads

Remove ornament top; place a feather and just a pinch of glitter inside
ornament; replace top. Paint a border of glue around the top of the
ornament; sprinkle with glitter and seed beads. Set aside to dry.

Magical Bubbles

12 1/2" dia. clear glass or
    acrylic ornaments

hot glue gun with glue
12 mini tin candle clip-ons

Remove and discard hangers from ornaments; coat ornament tops
with glue. Turn upside down and insert glued tops into clip-ons; set
aside to dry. Clip onto tree at ends of branches, to resemble bubbles
that have just floated down.

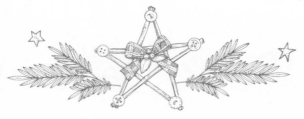

Wish Upon a Star

Stars hanging here and there and everywhere add magic and sparkle to every holiday get-together.

Star-bound Cedar Wreath

3 to 5 ft. gold or silver bead
    garland
desired size cedar wreath
24 gold or silver chenille stems

3 4" dia. wooden stars with
    pre-drilled holes for hanging
white acrylic paint

Loop bead garland loosely through center and around the bottom of the wreath several times; set aside. Paint stars white; set aside to dry. Attach stars to the lower left-hand front side of the wreath, spacing each several inches apart. Make 3 fanned-out bundles of 8 chenille stems apiece; wire one bundle behind each star, making a starry trail for each star. Hang up wreath and enjoy!

✳ Deck the Halls ✩

A Starry Tree for Outdoors

8"x10" sheet of thin plastic or
  heavy cardboard
cardboard
assorted prepasted wallpaper
paper punch

wire ornament hooks
balled evergreen tree
large sled, half barrel or
  galvanized tub

Draw a star of the desired size and trace onto plastic; cut out. Use plastic template to cut out desired number of stars from cardboard; set aside. Cut out twice that number of stars from prepasted wallpaper. Moisten wallpaper; adhere one wallpaper star to each side of every cardboard star. Set aside to dry. Place a balled evergreen tree in the desired holder (sled, half barrel or tub). Punch a hole in each star; use wire ornament hooks to hang stars all over the tree. Direct a spotlight for a starry night presentation.

Accordion Stars

8-1/2"x11" sheet cardstock-
  weight gold paper
ruler
8-inch length 26-gauge wire

craft glue
double-sided tape

Cut a 6"x3" strip of gold paper; fold into 1/2-inch pleats, accordion style, along the 6-inch edge. Wrap wire around center of pleated strip; twist ends together to secure. Trim both ends of pleated strips into a petal shape; open into a round star, taping edges that meet. Attach with wire to wreath, tree or centerpiece as desired.

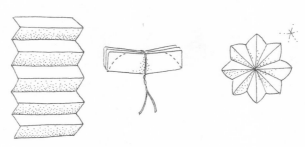

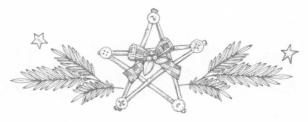

Cranberry Craze

These ruby red wonders add touches of country Christmas wherever they are hung.

Cranberry Star

2 lengths 22-gauge wire, one a few inches longer than the other

fresh cranberries
florist's wire
raffia

Thread cranberries on wires; lay side-by-side and bend into a star shape with the shorter of the 2 wires toward the inside. Connect wire points with florist's wire as well as wire joins. Wrap raffia between pairs of cranberries, one on each wire to bind both stars together. Add a raffia bow at top of star and hang outdoors.

Deck the Halls ✰

Cranberry Strands

quilting needle
natural-colored quilting thread
fresh cranberries

cinnamon sticks, cut to 1-inch
lengths
fresh kumquats

Thread the needle with a workable length thread, about 36 to
48 inches; knot one end. String in the following order: cranberry,
cinnamon stick, cranberry, kumquat, repeating until thread is full.
String kumquats lengthwise from end-to-end and cinnamon sticks
through the hollow part of the center. Arrange on tree, taking care fruit
does not rest on lights.

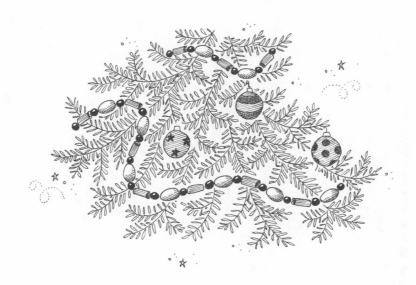

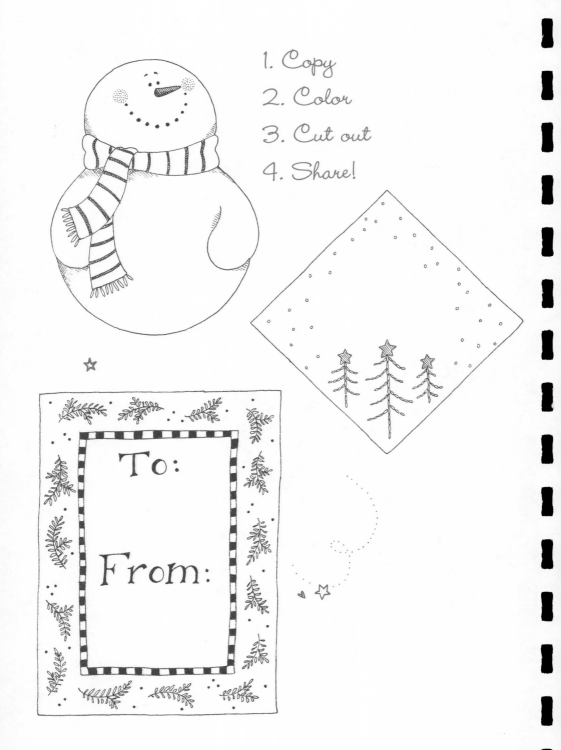

1. Copy
2. Color
3. Cut out
4. Share!

To:

From:

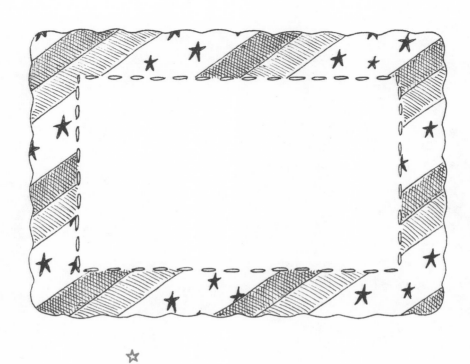

Ho

Ho

Ho

for:

from:

to:

from:

Use this recipe card to share all your favorite holiday recipes!

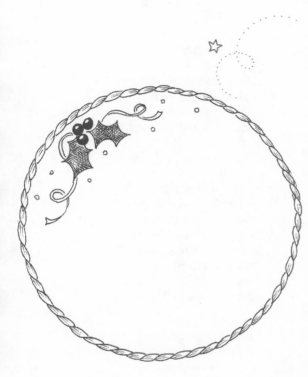

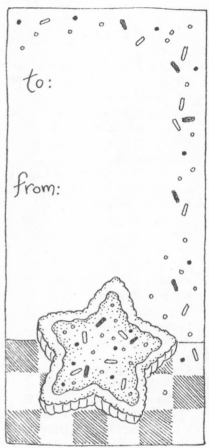

to:

from:

Enjoy sharing these cute
tags with
friends & family!

Sweet!

Index

Index

Index

We've cooked up a whole collection of Gooseberry Patch® books!

Have a taste for more? Call us toll-free at

1-800-854-6673

We'll send you our latest catalog filled with snowmen, Santas, ornaments, candles, cookie cutters, gourmet goodies, calendars, giftwrap, pottery, collectibles and MORE...including our best-selling cookbooks!

Phone us:
1·800·854·6673

Fax us:
1·740·363·7225

Visit our website:
www.gooseberrypatch.com

Send us your favorite recipe!

*and the memory that makes it special for you!** If we select your recipe for a brand new **Gooseberry Patch** cookbook, your name will appear right along with it...and you'll receive a FREE copy of the book! Mail to:

Vickie & Jo Ann
Gooseberry Patch, Dept. Book
600 London Road
Delaware, Ohio 43015

*Please include the number of servings and all other necessary information!

woolly mittens ❤ garlands of green 🌿 pine.

Scented memories ☆ new-fallen snow ✳ twinkly lights 💡 holiday cheer 🔔

sparkling tinsel ✳ peppermint swirls ☆

jolly gingerbread men 🍪 scrumptious sweets 🍬 holiday cheer ☕